REVISED EDITION

MODERN HARMONY

IN ITS

THEORY AND PRACTICE

BY

ARTHUR FOOTE A.M.

AND

WALTER R. SPALDING A.M.

Professor of Music at Harvard University

PRICE **$1.50** net

THE ARTHUR P. SCHMIDT CO.

BOSTON
120 BOYLSTON STREET

NEW YORK
8 WEST 40TH ST.

PREFACE

THE title of this work indicates the aim of the authors. Not a few statements and rules have been current in text-books that, from the point of view of composers and of the best teachers to-day, are unnecessary and sometimes even incorrect. When we find a rule constantly broken by one great composer after another, it is probable that the rule ought to be modified or given up, and not that the composers are wrong. It is the intention that statements and rules in this book shall be expressed with exact truth, and explained when real explanation is possible. It has also been remembered that better work is secured by directions as to what may be done, than by laying too much stress upon what is forbidden.

About some matters there is a marked difference of opinion among theorists; such things cannot be considered as settled for good and all, and no definite statement should be made excluding other well-grounded points of view, *e.g.* the chords of the 11th and 13th.

The chord of the 6th has been treated with more detail than usual, an attempt having been made to analyze and classify the features that make this chord so difficult for the student.

While the old strict rules as to secondary 7ths are given fully, the modern theory and use of these chords have received just consideration.

The chord of the 9th has been discussed as a largely independent chord; it was also obvious that the growing feeling about chords of the 11th and 13th ought to be recognized, although the opinion of the authors, as explained in the chapter on that subject, is that these latter can seldom be classified as independent chords.

It is believed that the treatment of chromatic alterations in chords, and of the augmented 6th, 6–5 and 6–4–3 chords is in accordance with present thought, and that this is also the case as regards suspension.

The chapter on the old modes is necessarily brief, but it is hoped that it may lead the student to further investigation of an important and interesting question.

It is often the case that exercises with figured basses are written correctly, but only mathematically, by simply reckoning each chord as a kind of puzzle, without reflecting that the whole thing means music after

43632

all. The most difficult thing, for one not used to it, is the having a mental conception of the real sounds of the symbols written down — in other words, hearing with the eye. Education now is directed to the thing, not to the symbol. As the practical way of working in that direction, in this book from the very beginning the harmonizing of melodies goes step by step with the writing from figured basses. It is hoped that the illustrations quoted from many composers will be of help by showing what has actually been done with our harmonic material.

For matters connected with acoustics (§§ 5, 13), the student is referred to Helmholtz's book "On the Sensations of Tone," and to the essay on "Partial Tones" in Grove's "Dictionary of Music."

Boston, *August*, 1905.

TABLE OF CONTENTS

HARMONY

CHAPTER I

INTERVALS

1. THE study of Harmony — the Grammar of Music — begins with the subject of Intervals, for as soon as we consider even two different tones there must be some method of determining their relationship. An Interval is the measurement of the *difference in pitch* between any two tones, whether they are sounded together and stand in a harmonic relationship, or in succession and are used melodically.

2. Notes refer to the written symbols — the notation of music — and are apprehended by the eye; tones refer to sounds, which must be accurately determined and keenly felt by the ear. A careful study of intervals helps greatly toward the acquisition of that clearness of thought and coöperation of eye and ear absolutely indispensable to the well-trained musician.

3. Every interval has a two-fold name, general and specific; *i.e.* an interval is a third, a fourth, a fifth, etc., and also a third, a fourth, or a fifth, of a *certain kind*; *e.g.* a major third, a perfect fourth, a diminished fifth, etc.

4. The general numerical name of an interval is always determined by counting inclusively, from the lower note to the higher, the number of lines and spaces involved. As lines and spaces (the scale-degrees) are designated by the letters of the alphabet from A to G in order, a simple rule is this: — *Always reckon intervals by letters.* The interval C-E is always a *third*, there being *three* degrees (C, D, E), no matter how either C or E may be qualified by accidentals (sharps, flats, and naturals).[1] The following intervals, for instance, are all thirds:

although not all of the same kind. Likewise C-F♯ is a certain kind of *fourth* (C, D, E, F); C-G♭ a certain kind of *fifth* (C, D, E, F, G).

---

[1] The sign ♮ ought logically to be called a cancel, as its office is exclusively to cancel the sharp or flat that would otherwise be in force.

5. Exactness in thinking and writing intervals is of the utmost consequence, for it is the same thing as spelling words correctly; moreover
we shall find later that different intervals have different resolutions, the
chords of which they form a part being different, *e.g.*

Most persons have only such a conception of intervals as is derived from
familiarity with the pianoforte keyboard, the result being often an entirely wrong way of looking at the matter. Since for practical reasons
there is but one key of the pianoforte for both F♯ and G♭, it at first
naturally seems that the notes F♯ and G♭ must be identical, while really
they differ in pitch, when played in perfect tune on a stringed instrument.
This can be perceived by an acute ear, if the two tones are sounded simultaneously; F♯ is higher in pitch than G♭ by a very small interval called
the "Comma of Pythagoras," which is about one quarter of a semitone.
Tones which differ in notation, but sound alike on a keyed instrument,
are said to have an enharmonic relationship.

DVOŘÁK, Requiem

6. The *general* kind of any interval being thus determined by counting
the number of letters in their order, we must next find what is its *specific*
name. For this purpose intervals are classified as Perfect, Major, Minor,
Augmented, and Diminished. (In chromatically altered chords, doubly augmented and doubly diminished intervals are also found.) The need for
these more precise definitions will be clearly seen if, before going further,
we examine for a moment the modern scale-system.

7. A scale consists of a succession of tones arranged according to a definite plan.[1] Our major diatonic scale, for instance, is a succession of seven different tones (hence called a heptatonic scale),[2] so arranged that between any two degrees there is always a whole tone, with the exception of the interval between the third and fourth, where there is a semitone (also between the seventh and eighth (or 8ve.)).

It will be seen that the eighth tone or *octave* is merely a repetition of the first one at a different pitch; at this octave the series recommences. The term "diatonic" means *throughout the tones,* or degrees, of the scale; hence a *diatonic* scale is one in which there is *one note,* neither more nor less, on *each* degree of the staff, *i.e.* on each line and space in succession.[3] Every musical person has received this succession of tones as part of his musical inheritance, *i.e.* he can sing it without effort when asked, and readily recognizes it when heard.

8. If the intervals of the above scale be examined, it is evident that those which have the same *general* name are not always of the same size and by no means of the same effect: for instance, the intervals C-E and A-C are both thirds, but of a different variety. If the tones C, E are sounded several times;

---

[1] If it were not for the traditional and convenient arrangement of keys on the pianoforte keyboard, we should probably have at least *nineteen* keys in an octave — c, c♯, d♭, d, d♯, e♭, e, e♯, f, f♯, g♭, g, g♯, a♭, a, a♯, b♭, b, b♯, — instead of the *twelve* black and white keys. Violinists have to do with all these tones in practical playing. Many compositions of imperfectly educated writers are defaced by a kind of misspelling which comes from ignorance of intervals; the student should feel it to be of equal importance to spell both music and language correctly.

[2] During the evolution of music many kinds of scales have been in use among different nations, some of which we shall mention later.

[3] It is well to realize this, for we often find the Pentatonic scale of five tones, which is not a diatonic scale, but contains steps of more than a tone, *e.g.*

The student can invent melodies based on this scale by using the black keys of the pianoforte.

and then, after a pause, the notes

every one will feel the striking difference between these thirds. The interval A-C is called a *minor* or lesser third (containing a tone and a half) in comparison with the interval C-E, which is a *major* or greater third (containing two whole tones). Of the seven seconds contained within the scale, five are *major* (containing one whole tone), C-D, D-E, etc., whereas two are *minor* (containing a semitone), E-F and B-C. Likewise in regard to the other intervals: C-F is one kind of a fourth, and F-B is another; the sixth C-A is larger than the sixth E-C; the seventh C-B sounds very different from the seventh D-C.

9. From the above considerations it is evident that the classification of intervals as seconds, thirds, fifths, etc., is not sufficient; there must be some more precise nomenclature to show their exact nature, *i.e.* what *kind* of a second, third, etc. In learning to apply the specific terms, Perfect, Major, Minor, Augmented, and Diminished, the easiest way to begin is to recognize this fact: — that in every major scale the intervals having the tonic (key-note) for their lowest tone are either major or perfect, *e.g.*

10. *Minor* intervals, as may be inferred from the name, are a semitone smaller than their corresponding majors. A major interval is changed into a minor either by raising the lower note, or by lowering the upper one a chromatic [2] semitone. Thus C-E is a major third; C♯-E and C-E♭ are both minor thirds. In forming minor thirds be sure that the *general* interval of a third is preserved. C-D♯,

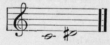

for instance, as the notes are on adjacent degrees, is not a *third* at all, but a *second*.

---

[1] The unison (two voices singing the same tone) cannot strictly be called an interval, but for convenience is so named. When one of its tones, however, is raised or lowered chromatically, we do get a real interval.

[2] A chromatic semitone is one in which both notes are on the same degree of the staff, *e.g.* C-C♯; a diatonic semitone one between notes on adjoining degrees, *e.g.* C-B or C-D♭.

11. An *augmented* interval is a chromatic semitone larger than a perfect or a major interval. It is obvious that an interval may be augmented either by raising the upper note or by lowering the lower. Thus D-G being a perfect fourth, either D-G♯ or D♭-G will be an augmented fourth. The augmented intervals starting on C are as follows:

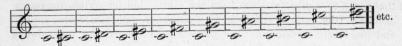

These augmented intervals are all usable; augmented 4ths, 5ths, 6ths, and, in a somewhat less degree, 2ds, are of frequent appearance in harmony. Augmented 3ds, 7ths, and 8ves have no harmonic value, although occasionally found as passing tones, *e.g.*

12. A *diminished* interval is a chromatic semitone less than a perfect or a minor. As in the cases given above, it is immaterial which of the two tones composing the original interval be altered; *e.g.* C-G being a perfect 5th, either C♯-G or C-G♭ is a diminished fifth. The diminished intervals are:

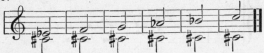

a diminished unison is unthinkable, and the diminished 2d and 9th are of no practical use:

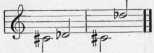

in the diminished 6th, the lower tone may occur as a passing tone; *e.g.*

Diminished 3ds, 4ths, 5ths,[1] and 7ths, especially the last, occur frequently and are of great harmonic use.

13. From the above illustrations it will be seen that major and minor, augmented and diminished intervals explain themselves and are readily understood. The student, however, is often at a loss to appreciate the appropriateness of the term *perfect*, as applied to unisons, 4ths, 5ths, and 8ves, and to *these only*. To most hearers the 3d is probably the most satisfactory of all intervals when sounded alone, and yet we are told that it is not perfect, while the 4th is called by that name, although much less agreeable by itself than the third. These perfect intervals have been given that name to *distinguish* them from the others, and for certain reasons in acoustics (**the** ratio of vibration, for example, in each case is very simple, and practically *invariable*). The perfect octave above any tone always has just *twice* the number of vibrations in the same time as that tone; *i.e.* the ratio of the interval of the perfect octave is 1 : 2, whereas major and minor thirds and sixths, as the student will understand more clearly, when he comes to know about equal temperament and methods of tuning, have not such simple ratios, and often vary considerably in character. These perfect intervals also differ from all the others in that they *remain perfect when inverted* (as will be seen later).

14. Before explaining *Inversions* it will be necessary to define and explain two terms of great significance in the classification of intervals.

---

[1] A diminished interval when made still smaller by a semitone, becomes *doubly diminished; e.g.*

FRANZ. (Song)

In like manner an augmented interval becomes *doubly augmented* when made a semitone larger: *e.g.*

These intervals are not available in simple chord-formations.

These terms are *Consonance* and *Dissonance*, and from the outset the student should have a broad idea of their meaning. We are prone to think of a consonance as something which *sounds well*, and of a dissonance as being *harsh* and *discordant*; but in a harmonic sense the import of the terms is far wider. A *consonance* is a combination of two tones that in itself produces a more or less satisfactory effect, *i.e.* is complete, independent, and does not arouse in the hearer the feeling that some other combination must follow. For example, if any one of the following inter-vals is played (of course with pauses between), it will be evident that each is satisfactory and *can stand by itself* (*i.e.* it need not be approached in any particular way, and arouses no expectations of a subsequent interval).

Henceforth the following intervals are to be classified and considered as *consonances*: — Perfect Octaves, Perfect Unisons, Perfect Fourths, and Perfect Fifths, and also Major and Minor Thirds and Sixths. Upon analysis it will be seen that each of the above intervals is one of the consonances enumerated. In like manner *chords* composed only of consonant intervals are independent, satisfactory in themselves, *i.e.* they may both begin and end a sentence, giving an effect of stability, or even, if used too much, of inertia. This will be felt, if each of the following chords is played, of course with appropriate pauses.

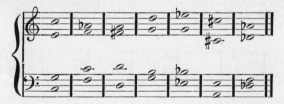

15. A *Dissonance*, on the other hand, is a combination of two tones, which in itself produces an impression of *incompleteness*; it is unsatisfactory, dependent, so that the hearer urgently feels that something must follow before a logical pause can be made. Play on the pianoforte each one of the following intervals, pausing, as before, after each.

Each of these intervals is unsatisfactory *by itself*, and depends, for a complete effect, upon something else to follow. We now place after each of

these dissonances a consonance, and the *combination* of a *dissonance* followed
by a *consonance* is felt to be entirely satisfactory.

The *dissonances* then are *all* forms of 2ds, 7ths, and 9ths and *all* augmented
and diminished intervals; in like manner, a *dissonant chord* is one which
contains at least ONE dissonance (not necessarily very harsh), and, taken
by itself, has an incomplete effect.   Play each one of the following dissonant
chords, and the impression of incompleteness, or suspense, is plainly felt.[1]

We now follow each of these dissonant chords with a consonant chord, and
the feeling of rest and satisfaction is evident at once.

16. The consonance following the dissonance is called the *Chord
of Resolution* (the laws by which dissonances are appropriately resolved
are fully explained later).   Consonance is a point of *rest*, and dissonance of
unrest.   All music, in a broad sense, consists of a happy combination of
these two complementary elements; too much of either is fatal, for excessive consonance produces stagnation, while too many dissonances often
result in irritation and undue restlessness.   Dissonances in music furnish

[1] The student should analyze and name each one of the dissonant intervals found therein.

an element of motion, of progress, and keep the mind and imagination of the hearer aroused. In certain of the above resolutions the feeling of rest and satisfaction is stronger than in others, and oftentimes more than a single chord is needed to resolve a dissonance satisfactorily. A dissonance, also, does not always resolve at once, one often proceeding to another, in order that the feeling of suspense and of striving may be prolonged.

17. An interval is said to be *inverted* when the relative position of the two notes is changed, either by placing the lower note an octave higher or the upper one an octave lower.

Thus F-C is a perfect 5th: if F be placed above C, or C below F, in either case the result is a perfect 4th.

Every Unison (1) on inversion becomes an Octave (8).
" 2d " " " a 7th.
" 3d " " " " 6th.
" 4th " " " " 5th.
" 5th " " " " 4th.
" 6th " " " " 3d.
" 7th " " " " 2d.
" Octave (8) " " " " Unison (1).

Major intervals on inversion become Minor.
Minor " " " " Major.
Augmented " " " " Diminished.
Diminished " " " " Augmented.

But *Perfect Intervals always remain Perfect;* it is thus seen, as said before, that the perfect intervals (unisons, 4ths, 5ths, and 8ves) differ from all others in not changing their *specific* kind on inversion.

18. The student should now verify the above statements by a careful analysis of the following table.

19. The following exercises are to be worked out: —

(1) Write the names of the following intervals; indicate those that are consonant by (*C*), those that are dissonant by (*D*).

A good method of procedure is the following: — *Invariably* find the *general* name of the interval first (*i.e.* whether it is a 3d, 5th, 6th, etc.) by counting the number of degrees, inclusively; *e.g.* (*a*) above is some kind of a fifth, for D-A includes five scale-degrees, (e) is a second, (*k*) is a third, etc. When possible consider the lower note of the interval as the key-note of a major scale, and remember that the successive degrees of the major scale form, with the *key-note* of the same, either *perfect* or *major* intervals; *i.e.* the 1st, 4th, 5th, and 8ve are perfect, and the 2d, 3d, 6th and 7th, are major. Then observe how these numerical intervals are altered (made larger or smaller) by the use of accidentals. When the lower note is not the key-note of any ordinary scale, it is well to consider what the interval would be, if free from accidentals; *e.g.*, D-A is a perfect fifth; if the lower note is raised, the interval is lessened by a semitone and therefore is a diminished fifth.

(2) Write (and afterwards play) the following intervals: a minor second of E, of B♭ and of F; a diminished third of C♯, E, and B♭; an augmented fourth of F♯, D♭, and C♯; an augmented 6th of F♭, of A, and of B♭; a diminished seventh of E♯, F✕, and C.

20. Considerable attention has been paid to this subject of intervals, and the above exercises should be worked out faithfully and patiently. Although the mistake is sometimes made of considering this work formal and dry, it must be undertaken and conquered. A quick, clear insight into the nature of intervals is as necessary for the subsequent study of harmony, as is the multiplication table for the study of mathematics. Let systematic attention be paid to quickness and accuracy of ear, and gradually the two-fold power will be gained of *hearing* with the *eye* and *seeing* with the *ear*; *i.e.* when any interval is seen, the musician should hear it (to himself) and be able to *sing* it, and conversely when an interval is heard, it should be possible to visualize it and to write it down in *correct notation*. The student [1] is not expected to recognize at once all the more complicated intervals, but from the outset a definite attempt should be made to *realize* in *sound* major and minor 3ds, the perfect and the diminished 5th, the perfect and the augmented 4th, and the three 7ths, major, minor, and diminished.

---

[1] The teacher can likewise add considerable interest to this work, by selecting certain well-known melodies illustrating the various intervals. For instance, the beginning of Wagner's "Flying Dutchman" Overture shows a striking use of the perfect 5th; the main theme of Beethoven's 3d "Leonore" Overture contains several augmented 4ths, etc.

CHAPTER II

THE SCALES

21. BEFORE we treat of chords and their combinations, something must be learned of the evolution [1] and formation of our modern scales, major, minor, and chromatic. The scale gets its name from an analogy to the steps of a ladder (Latin *scala*). All nations that have made music have agreed in adopting some selection of tones as a scale, although the same series has not by any means been used by all. Any succession of tones may be said to form a scale, and these tones may be smoothly connected (diatonically), or skips may appear between certain of them. During the history of music there have actually been in use scales of three, four, five, six, seven tones and more. All musical peoples, however, appear to have appreciated the intimate natural relationship between tones lying that distance apart which we call an *octave*; the differences are in the intermediate steps. In modern music we employ a series of *seven* steps, called the diatonic scale, with the power of interposing certain intermediate chromatic steps. The *major* diatonic scale, then, is as follows:

(For the definition see Chapter I, **7.**) The pattern of the major scale is fixed, and there is but one form, the same for all major keys.

22. The formation of the minor diatonic scale is as follows:

The first and most important characteristic of the minor scale is the minor third between the key-note and the third degree. The half-steps are between the 2d and 3d, 5th and 6th, and 7th and 8th degrees, while between the 6th and 7th degrees is the striking interval of a step and a half — an

---

[1] Historically considered the growth of modern scales and of chords went on at the same time, each reacting upon the other; but from our present point of view we shall explain chords as being founded upon the successive degrees of accepted scale systems. Those who desire more knowledge on this very important and interesting subject are advised to read the second chapter of Parry's "Evolution of the Art of Music," and also the article on the Greek Modes in Grove's "Dictionary of Music."

augmented 2d. The minor scale in distinction from the major has
an elastic scheme, and appears in *three* forms ascending and *three* descending, as follows:

(a), (b), (d) and (f) are the forms chiefly used in chord formation; (c) and (f) are much used
melodically, but are obviously not characteristic, being only the relative major scale begun
on a different tone; (b) is also much used melodically, but (e) is seldom found in modern music,
although it was often employed by Bach and his contemporaries.[1]

The minor scale, it will be observed, always begins with a minor third.

23. Theoretically, scales may begin upon any tone chosen, and
conformation made to the above patterns by the introduction of *appropriate accidentals*; *i.e.* there may be major and minor scales on C, C♯, D,
D♯, E, E♯, etc. Practically only a certain number of these scales is in common use, for some of them would contain so many accidentals as to make
the reading of the notes difficult.[2] As to the formation of scales in practical use, experiment showed that if a scale were begun on the *fifth* degree
of the above scale of C major, the same series of notes could be used and
the same combination of tones and semitones would result with one exception, *e.g.*

The F, the seventh degree, or *leading-tone*, as we shall call it later, has to
be raised a semitone to preserve the same relativity of tones and semi-

---

[1] In Bach's "Chromatic Fantasie" will be found striking instances of the manner
in which different forms of the same minor scale are used in the same passage.

[2] In complicated chromatic modulations, however, we sometimes find, for a few measures, chords written in very extreme keys. For instance, near the beginning of Liszt's song
to Goethe's "Mignon," there is a passage in the key of A♯ major. No one, however, would
begin a composition in A♯ major, for the enharmonic B♭ (A♯ = B♭) with two flats in the
signature is far easier to read than A♯, the key of ten sharps. Compare also the opening
measures of Schumann's "Carnaval" for chords written in the key of F♭ major (8 flats)
instead of the enharmonic E major (4 sharps).

tones as in the scale of C major. The other sharp keys are formed in like manner. The formula may be stated as follows: — to construct *major* scales by the introduction of *sharps*, begin in each case with the *fifth* degree of the old scale and raise the *seventh* degree of the new scale a *semitone*, continuing till *every* one of the *seven different* tones has been sharped, *e.g.*

In actual music it is not customary to write the sharps or flats in connection with each note; they are grouped together at the beginning of the piece and form what is known as the *signature*, being placed in order from left to right on the scale-degrees influenced in any given case. The signatures of the different sharp keys are as follows:

24. If this series be continued, the next key-notes in order will be G♯, D♯, A♯, E♯, and B♯. But as all these keys involve the use of double sharps — the signature of B♯ major, for instance, would be

— in practically every case it is more convenient to use the *enharmonic-flat* scale. With B♯ major, the enharmonic of C major, the series closes; for we have now completed the "circle of fifths," as it is termed, going through the sharp keys with ascending perfect fifths. The circle may be represented as follows:

Read around to the right.

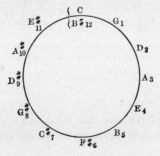

25. The flat scales are formed in succession by an analogous proceeding; *i.e.* starting with C major, if a new scale is begun in every case on the degree a perfect *fifth below*, the *normal* order of *tones* and *semitones* is preserved with the need of but one change, *e.g.*

That is, in the major scale starting on F, the fourth degree has to be *lowered* a semitone, that the series may conform to the established pattern. The other flat scales are formed in like manner; *i.e.* the key-notes *descend* by perfect fifths, and in every case the fourth degree of the new scale is to be lowered. The signatures of the different flat keys are as follows:

As in the case of sharp **keys,** the series might be continued, but as soon as double flats would be necessary the *enharmonic-sharp* key is preferred.

Read around to the left.

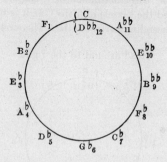

26. As keys which have more than six sharps or six flats are somewhat complicated in notation it is customary to use the simpler enharmonic, *i.e.*

B (5 sharps) instead of C♭ (7 flats) and likewise D♭ (5 flats) instead of C♯ (7 sharps). This will be made clear by the following circle of keys:

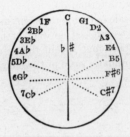

It is therefore evident that *twelve* major scales are commonly employed, and as we shall soon see that every major scale has its relative minor, *twenty-four* [1] major and minor scales are commonly held to be the basis of our harmonic system.

27. The minor scale is composed of the same tones (with one exception) as is the corresponding major scale to which it is said to be *related*, and its tonic is a minor third below that of the latter; the one tone different in the two scales is so because of the fact that the so-called *leading-tone* in every major and minor scale is a semitone below the tonic. The evident relationship of these major and minor scales, and the single difference that exists between them are shown thus.

(If the seventh degree (leading-tone) be not raised chromatically, one of the most characteristic features of the scale is lost.)

The above scale, with an augmented second between the 6th and 7th degrees, is called the *harmonic* minor scale, in distinction from various

---

1 It may serve as an aid to memory to recall the fact that J. S. Bach's work, the "Well-Tempered Clavichord," is often referred to as the "48 Preludes and Fugues": that is, two preludes and two fugues were composed for each of the set of twelve major and twelve minor keys. In Beethoven's "Zwei Präludien durch alle Dur-Tonarten," op. 39, will be found an example of modulation through all the major keys.

forms chiefly used for melodic purposes (see Chapter II, **22**). Many important and necessary facts will be learned when we come to speak of the chords formed on the degrees of the minor scale and begin to write exercises in that mode. At present we have only touched upon the main points with reference to scale-formation.

28. The *chromatic* scale, so important in modern music, melodically and also harmonically, is composed entirely of half-steps, *i.e.* it includes the twelve semitones to be found within the octave. The grammatically correct notation of the chromatic scale of C would be as follows:

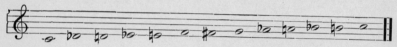

a different notation, however, is often used, being somewhat easier to read on account of the fewer accidentals.

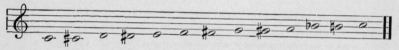

In writing the chromatic scale, composers have been uncertain and careless in the employment of the necessary accidentals; in Beethoven's pianoforte concerto in G major, for example, the chromatic scale being written in four different ways.

It might be argued that sharps should be employed in an ascending scale, and flats in a descending one; but, on the other hand, the following examples would look absurd and be illogical as written.

The best notation of the chromatic scale in any given case is a point as to which no specific directions can be given; common sense and experience must decide.

29. In preparation for the formation of chords, it is necessary to become familiar with the technical names of the various scale-degrees in distinction from the mere numerical designation of 2d, 3d, etc., especially as the derivation of these terms conveys much meaning. The first tone popularly known as the key-note, is called the *Tonic*: this is an abbreviation of the Latin *Tonica*, and means the Tone, *i.e.*, the *chief tone* with which the scale begins, and to which each one of the other tones (both diatonic and chromatic) bears a definite relationship. A similar term is Tonality, the full import of which will be understood when we come to learn about the principal chords in a key. The most important tone after the tonic is the fifth, called the *Dominant*, on account of its ruling influence upon the key. The fourth tone of the scale is called the *Sub-Dominant* or lower dominant, because it lies the same distance below the tonic that the dominant lies above it. On this point the student should be perfectly clear from the outset; every tonic has *two* dominants, one a *perfect fifth above*, called the *dominant*, the other a *perfect fifth below*, called the *sub-* or *under-dominant*. The chart makes this clear.

Tonic. Dominant.

Sub-Dom-inant.

The sub-dominant is never to be explained as being so called because it is the tone below the dominant. The third tone is called the *Mediant*, as it is midway between the tonic and the dominant. In like manner the sixth tone is called the *Sub-Mediant*, or lower mediant, as it is midway between the sub-dominant and tonic.

Tonic. Dominant.

Mediant.

Sub-Mediant.

Sub-Dom-inant.

The second tone of the scale is called the *Super-Tonic*, *i.e.* the one above the tonic. The seventh tone, on account of its tendency to *rise* or *lead up* to the tonic, is called the *Leading-Tone*.[1] This is the most important of a class called *Tendency Tones*, and great care is always to be exercised in its treatment.

[1] The French term for this seventh degree of the scale is "la note sensible," *i.e.* the sensitive note.

CHAPTER III

TRIADS

30. HAVING now defined intervals and their inversions, and stated the main facts in regard to scales, we come to the construction of chords, and the manner of their connection. A chord, in its uninverted form, is a combination of three or more tones, each of them being either a major or minor third above the tone below it. Combinations of *three* different tones are called *Triads*, and consist of a low tone and the third and fifth above. Chords of four different tones are called *Seventh chords*, and are merely triads with an additional tone, *i.e.* 1, 3, 5, 7.[1] The most convenient name for the tone on which any uninverted chord is founded is the ROOT, a term always to be understood as having that meaning, the lowest tone of other (inverted) chords being called the *bass*. Triads appear in many forms in accordance with the specific varieties of the thirds and fifths; for example the following chords are all triads.

31. A triad with a *perfect* fifth and a *major* third is called a MAJOR TRIAD (Ex. *a*); with a *perfect* fifth and a *minor* third, a MINOR TRIAD (Ex. *b*). All other triads, DIMINISHED (Ex. *c, e*), AUGMENTED (Ex. *d*), are dissonant in their nature and require careful treatment. Our first exercises will consist largely of major and minor triads.

32. On each of the seven tones in every major and minor scale there can be erected a triad. Those on the degrees of the major scale are as follows:

Of this series the tonic, dominant and sub-dominant triads are major (hence marked with a large Roman numeral). The triads on the second,

---

[1] The series may be continued by thirds to chords of the ninth, and even in some cases to chords of the eleventh and thirteenth, *e.g.*

third, and sixth degrees are minor (small numerals), and that on the leading-tone diminished (VII°). (This last triad will be sparingly used until we
come to inverted chords.) The triads on I, V, and IV, are the most important, as they have a close connection with each other, and when used in
combination always define clearly the tonality.

33. Triads, and in fact all chords, have a natural connection when
they have a tone or more in common; the following chart shows the relationship of the three principal triads.

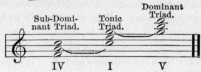

Triads with two tones in common have a particularly close relationship;
this happens when their roots are a third apart. Triads on adjoining degrees of the scale have obviously no common tone.

34. Our first exercises are to be simple combinations of chords for
four voices, soprano, alto, tenor, bass.[1] The usual compass of the voices
may be set as follows, although for solo singers these limits are frequently
exceeded.

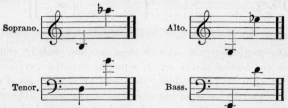

35. As there are but three tones in triads, and we have four voices,
it is necessary that in every chord one of the tones shall be doubled, being
sung by two voices. *As a general thing, the most satisfactory result is obtained*

---

[1] For the present the normal relative position of these four voices is to be preserved,
and they are not allowed to cross each other (soprano below alto, alto below tenor, bass above
tenor) *e.g.*

The musical effect resulting from the crossing of voices *can* be very good, but will not
be so unless planned by a writer of experience and taste; the student must absolutely
avoid it.

by doubling the root; the third is doubled when the leading of the voices brings that result about naturally and logically; the chord is less strong when the fifth is doubled [1], *bad voice-leading often also resulting.*

36. When the three upper voices (soprano, alto and tenor) lie within less than an octave, the harmony is said to be in *close position*, whether the bass be near the tenor or far removed; if the three upper voices are more evenly distributed, covering more than an octave, we have *open position;* when they cover exactly an octave, we may consider that we have either close or open position, being determined as to this point by the chords preceding or following. Wherever there is to be a wide interval between any of the voices it should be almost always between bass and tenor, and, excepting for an occasional chord, there should never be a larger interval than an octave between soprano and alto, or alto and tenor.

Whether in any particular case open or close position shall be employed will depend on the *leading* of the *voices,* sometimes on the mere sound of the chord, often again on practicability (for there are successions of chords that can be written effectively in but one kind cf position). The student is strongly advised to use *both positions* from the first, for only in this way can ease and pliability in part-writing be obtained. In many cases it is well to try both ways, and to cultivate the judgment by selecting the one preferable.

---

[1] As to doubling of the 3d, *cf.* pp. 29, 30, 41, 50. Doubling of the 5th sometimes results in such a disposition of the voices as to render good voice-leading impossible. In the following, *e.g.* the tenor produces consecutive 8ves by descending to F, and consecutive 5ths if it ascends to A; it is obvious that we must change the first chord and double its root.

With triads it is obvious that in every chord the root must be present, as that is the tone on which it is based. Without this we shall not know with what triad we have to do; the third must also be heard, as determining whether the triad be major or minor. In some cases it is not absolutely necessary to have the fifth, when the leading of the voices causes it to be naturally omitted, without our being doubtful whether the chord be a triad or not.

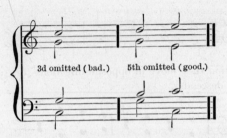

37. Here follow examples of different groupings of the triad C–E–G, to illustrate principles of *doubling* and *spacing*; each chord should be carefully played and the effect analyzed. It is to be understood that the relative position of the *upper* notes of a chord makes no difference in its nature, provided the *bass* be unchanged. In the following chords, **C, E, G** are the only different notes used, and in each, C, the *root* of the triad, is in the bass. In fact *all chords* in which the *root* is the *lowest* tone are said to be in "root (or fundamental) position" in distinction from inverted positions, of which we shall learn later.

38. In combining chords the two most important principles are these: 1st, the *melodic* progression of each single voice, and 2d, the *harmonic* progression of each part in its relationship to the others. A good melody is one that proceeds naturally and without awkward *skips*; hence melodies in general should be *diatonic* in character, although simple skips of 3ds, 4ths, 5ths, and 6ths, may be introduced for variety. In our early work no skips of a 7th or of any augmented or diminished interval are to be used:

the only exception to this being the diminished 5th, which may be introduced when one of the tones is the leading-tone; *e.g.*

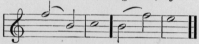

39. As regards harmonic progression, there are three kinds of part-motion. *Similar* motion occurs when voices move in the same direction; *e.g.*

in *contrary* motion they move in opposite directions (*i.e.* one part ascends, while the other descends),

and in *oblique* motion one voice stays on the same tone, while the other moves up or down.

40. It is evident that in four-part harmony ordinarily at least two [1] of these different kinds of motion must be combined.

[1] This does not apply where successive chords are mere changes in position;

we shall also meet later with chord successions in which *similar motion of all four voices* is of perfectly good effect, and often preferable or even necessary;

but *it must seldom be used in connecting different triads in root position.* When notes are tied (the tones prolonged in the same voices into the next chord), *the other voices may, it is true, proceed in similar motion,* though never in such a way as to produce consecutive 8ves or 5ths.

Triads whose roots are separated by a 3d, a 4th, a 5th, or a 6th, always have tones in common and may be naturally connected by a combination of *oblique* and *similar* motion. The common tones should largely be placed in the inner voices, in order that the soprano may have melodic movement and variety, *e.g.*

    I   V   I   IV   I   VI   I   III

41. Triads whose roots are on adjacent degrees of the scale *never have common tones, e.g.*

    V   IV   I   II

In connecting such triads we find that at least *two*, often *all*, of the *upper* voices are to be led in *contrary* motion to the bass, *e.g.*

    IV   V   IV   V   I   II

CONSECUTIVE OCTAVES AND FIFTHS

42. The first, and most important, absolute prohibition which we meet in composition is this: *consecutive 8ves, unisons, and 5ths are forbidden.*

That is: no two parts may *move* in perfect 8ves, unisons, or 5ths, with one another,[1] (*cf.* p. 106).

Voices are considered to be an 8ve or 5th apart, even when separated by more than one octave:

There is good reason for this. Taking CONSECUTIVE OCTAVES first, it is admitted *that they do not sound badly.* But it must be remembered that we are dealing with four independent voices, and if two of them go on singing the same tones, either in unison or an octave apart, we have practically reduced the number of different voices, as we hear them, to three. Moreover, the voices that double the melody stand out so conspicuously against their weaker companions (the latter not being doubled) that the proper balance is destroyed. On the other hand, when this very effect of a preponderance of one part is desired by a composer, he resorts to just such means; for instance, in the following choral from Mendelssohn, and in many of Beethoven's string-quartets.

MENDELSSOHN; Choral from "St. Paul"

etc.

[1] It may be asked why these octaves and fifths are prohibited, although found in the works of many great composers. The answer is simple; the student is not in a position to allow himself liberties that are only permissible to those who have experience and mature judgment.

BEETHOVEN; Op. 59, No. 1, (Scherzo)

Octaves, and fifths to a less degree, will be found in most chords in four-part harmony; these 8ves and 5ths are not *consecutive unless occurring between the same two* MOVING *voices in succession, e.g.*

(The student is to assure himself that this passage contains no *consecutive* octaves.)

43. With CONSECUTIVE FIFTHS the matter is different: *they often do sound badly.* The fact that certain composers have been skilful enough to manage them so that in particular cases they are satisfactory, is no argument that the inexperienced student may make experiments in that direction. He will probably fail, and had better not waste his time in trying.

The following example will roughly show varying degrees of badness and harmlessness as regards 5ths.

The triads (*a*) sound really ugly, largely because of the consecutive *major thirds.* The series (*b*) is not so harsh; and consecutive fifths are by no means infrequent in triads (*c*) which have tones in common. This is especially true of consecutive fifths between the tonic and dominant chords; *e.g.*

BEETHOVEN (Pastoral Symphony)

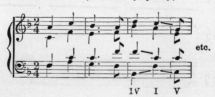

Successions like the following are often met with in instrumental music.

The following example from an Etude of Chopin, shows what a beautiful effect of mere sound can be produced, in part as a result of consecutive fifths.

In our early exercises the opportunity for unsatisfactory fifths will occur when triads on adjoining degrees are to be connected, as in this case the lack of a common tone causes a feeling of disjunction, and the prohibition of consecutive fifths must be strictly attended to.

Consecutive 8ves and 5ths can occur between any two voices, and in discussing the chord of the sixth, which follows naturally after the triad (being an inversion of it) we shall have to pay attention especially to the danger of such progressions occurring between soprano and alto, and alto and tenor. But for the present we are safe in confining our attention to consecutive 8ves and 5ths between the bass and any one of the other voices.

44. Before going on to other principles of chord connection, it will be well to say something of what is meant by the term "good leading of the parts." As most persons are acquainted with music chiefly as presented to them through the medium of the pianoforte, it is often a new idea that the different tones in such chords really belong to different voices, and that these voices, even in instrumental music (and always in vocal music), should have individual melodic movement.

This principle is not obvious in most pianoforte music, disguised as it is by the fact that other tones are often added to those representing the real voice parts, in order to obtain greater sonority, or a better quality of sound, or for some reason connected with the technical side of pianoforte writing.

CHOPIN, Nocturne Op. 9, No. 1

SCHUMANN, " Faschingsschwank," Op. 26

In the first illustration from Schumann, the number of notes in the chords varies for pianistic reasons; in the second, rests have been added (not indicated by the composer) to define more clearly the voice-parts; such rests are generally omitted for convenience in writing out pianoforte music.

45. In orchestral music the principle that voice-parts shall be real ones, having melodic value, is carried out so far as conditions permit, although necessary latitude is allowed in that so-called "filling in" voices are freely used when desired. A good illustration of adherence to strict part-writing will be found in the first movement of Beethoven's C minor symphony, and in Bach will be seen an almost unvarying employment of melodic part-writing in the orchestra; in string trios, quartets, etc., good part-writing is absolutely demanded.

It is well to say all this at first to confirm the student's mind in the idea that writing in real parts is eminently desirable in good music.

In all our work we shall consider ourselves as dealing with real voices, and therefore shall obviously have for a prime requisite *good and independent melodic movement of each voice.* If a choice be necessary, and there be a question whether the soprano or an inner voice (alto or tenor) shall be melodic, it is ordinarily the soprano that should have the preference; and we may state now that in the quartet of voices, soprano and bass are usually of most importance.

"Harvard Hymn"

JOHN KNOWLES PAINE

Compare these: soprano and bass, without the other voices, do not produce an entirely satisfying effect, but the result is *sense*, the hearer instinctively supplying what is felt to be missing. Without the soprano we are at a loss to know what is the melody; if we are not given the bass (*which determines the harmonies of the superstructure*) we can only guess at what that was intended to be. From this it is seen that *soprano and bass are the vital parts* of all chords, excepting that when the chief melody happens to be given to an inner part, alto or tenor, the soprano becomes of secondary importance. (Write out the above illustration with all four parts complete, and play it, comparing with what is given above.)

46. The seventh tone of the scale, always a semitone below the tonic, is of especial importance, since it is the only one that has of itself a distinct tendency to move in a particular direction. With our modern system of key tonality it has become an instinct for us to demand this rising of the 7th to the tonic; hence the name of *leading-tone*. Moreover, it is the essential factor in modulation, and, indeed, is almost always needed to fix a modulation with definiteness. Being a tone so very important and one naturally catching our attention quickly, it must not be over-emphasized, for it belongs to the class of so-called "sensitive" tones,[1] and therefore *must not be doubled* **as a rule.**

This accounts for the infrequent use of the triad on the 7th degree (in the fundamental position), for its *root*, which we should *naturally double*, is the *leading-tone*. N.B. Avoid the term *seventh* in speaking of the *leading-tone*, as later, when we have to do with CHORDS *of the seventh*, the two things easily become confused in one's mind.

This tendency of the leading-tone to ascend is particularly strong when it is the third of the dominant triad and the succeeding chord is the tonic triad, and is also more binding in connection with the soprano than with the inner voices, *e.g.*

When the dominant triad is followed by some other triad than the tonic, the leading-tone does not have such a strong tendency to ascend, *e.g.*

Although (*a*) is usually preferable to (*b*) and (*c*) to (*d*), for reasons which will be appreciated later.

---

[1] The leading-tone, the 7th in the chord of the seventh, and, in a less degree the 3d of the triad, may be called sensitive tones.

47. As consecutive 8ves and 5ths are nearly always [1] the result of similar motion, it is plain that in cases where they would occur because of that motion we can avoid them by employing contrary or oblique motion. We therefore combine our statements in the following rules for the connection of successive triads.

1. IF ONE OR MORE NOTES CAN BE TIED IN THE SAME VOICE OR VOICES (*i.e.* the tones prolonged into the next chord): EITHER — TIE WHATEVER NOTE OR NOTES CAN BE TIED, OR — LET THE SOPRANO, ALTO, AND TENOR MOVE IN THE OPPOSITE DIRECTION TO THE BASS. [2]

2. IF NO NOTES CAN BE TIED, THE 8VE AND 5TH MUST MOVE IN THE OPPOSITE DIRECTION TO THE BASS, THIS BEING VERY OFTEN THE CASE WITH THE 3D ALSO.

3. THE LEADING-TONE (WHICH IS ALMOST NEVER DOUBLED, *cf.* pp. 28, 36) USUALLY ASCENDS TO THE TONIC.

It is obvious (as regards rule 3) that if the leading-tone would make consecutive 5ths by ascending to the tonic, it must descend, contrary to its usual custom (see example (c) following). With the succession II–V in major keys (*cf.* §60), contrary motion is somewhat preferable:

[1] Consecutive 8ves and 5ths can also occur in contrary motion, being then open to the same objection as in similar motion (but see the top line of p. 74, and p. 242). A unison followed by an 8ve, or 8ve followed by unison, produces the same effect (p. 24) as consecutive 8ves.

[2] This is simply a workable rule and does not cover every possibility. If the bass descends a fifth, *e. g.* we may find similar motion of all four voices natural and suitable (*cf.* note on p. 22). In writing exercises it is well to indicate that a tone is kept in the same voice in two successive chords by writing a tie connecting the two notes, but in playing to disregard the tie.

V   VI

V   VI

(c)   (d)

48. In example (a) contrary motion is indicated for the succession II–V. It is not a point of great consequence; the reason for this preference lies mainly in the two consecutive major 3ds which would otherwise result between alto and tenor. The interval E♭–A, comprising three whole steps,

is called a TRITONE, the use of which was formerly forbidden ; although such a rule is needlessly rigid, there is no question but that the tritone demands expert handling. In this particular case we can justly say that the succession II–V which excludes it sounds better (cf. § 60.)[1]

In (b) the leading tone naturally ascends to the tonic, in whichever voice it may be, doubling the 3d in VI, in the succession V–VI (p. 41).

In (c) we see that the leading tone may be forced to descend, in order to avoid consecutive 5ths (in this case between soprano and bass).

In (d) is an instance of the leading tone descending (to the 5th of the triad), in order that the following chord may be complete. This is often of good effect with an inner voice (alto or tenor) in the succession V–I.

At page 253 will be found additional exercises, supplementing those on pp. 35, 37, 47, 65, 82, 92.

---

[1] For a more complete discussion of the matter, see Spalding's "Tonal Counterpoint." Chap. I, §§ 7–8.

CHAPTER IV

EXERCISES IN TRIADS

49. BEFORE proceeding to our first exercises, in connecting major triads and forming musical sentences, it is necessary to pay attention to certain details, which are considered in the following

GENERAL DIRECTIONS.

At present we shall use but two clefs:

remember always that we are dealing with four real voices, soprano, alto, tenor, and bass, **and** *write the soprano and alto* in the

clef, *tenor and bass* in the other.

In making notes have the stems of soprano and tenor to the right of the notes, pointed upward, with the tails (if any) turned to the right; the stems of the alto and bass to the left of the notes, pointed downward, with the tails turned to the right.

In the case of single notes on a staff, or of a group written as a chord — if the note is above the middle line, the stem will be on the left, pointed downward, and if below the middle line, on the right, pointed upward; with chords, similarly, the question of whether most of the notes are above or below the middle line determines the manner of writing.

Ties are to be made as follows, when two voices are on a staff:

i.e., curving upward when used with the upper notes, and downward when used with the lower notes.

50. Certain conventional signs have been for a long time used to define the meaning of what are called *figured basses* (*i.e.,* all basses other than triads in the fundamental position), where the other voices are not written out, and the chords are understood solely through the

figures and other signs employed. These figured basses were largely used in the organ parts **of** oratorios, etc., at the time of Bach and Händel, and with their assistance the player was **expect**ed to extemporize a full organ part.

51. In this book, if an 8 is below the *first* bass note of an exercise, or there is no figure, **the** soprano is to begin on the 8ve; if a 3 or 5 is below the first note, the soprano begins on the 3d or 5th.

A ♯ or ♮ under a bass note indicates that the 3d of the triad is to be chromatically **raised a** **half** step; this is done, *e.g.* with the dominant triad of the minor scale.

A ♯, ♭, or ♮, after a figure placed below a bass note, means that the note indicated by **the** figure is affected by that accidental; and a line drawn through a figure (₆, etc.) that the **note** indicated by that figure is to be chromatically raised. Any figures below a bass note mean that the chord is to be constructed by counting the intervals thus indicated upward from the bass. A figure 3 after any figure or combination of figures means that the chord first indicated is followed by a triad with the same bass note continued as its root. An 8 followed by a **7** indicates a triad followed by a chord of the 7th. A line—after a figure means that the note indicated by that figure is to be continued into the next chord.

(see chapter on 7ths)

In writing the next following exercises, remember that when the bass is given it is understood to be the root of a triad (*e.g.* the note C implies that the other notes of the chord are E and G). When the soprano is given it is either root, third, or fifth of the triad as the case may be; the bass to be written must always be the root of whatever triad is chosen.

52. *Write exercises without the aid of an instrument.* *After writing* try to realize, by singing and playing, how the single voices move and sound melodically, as well as in relation to the chords of which they form a part. Also listen carefully in playing the exercises over, that the ear may be trained by degrees to recognize chord progressions and the leading of the voices. The corrections made by the student himself, from a comparison of what he thinks is the sound that he writes down, and the real sound that he afterwards hears, is of more value than any changes suggested by another person.

53. Naturalness and simplicity are desirable in constructing our first chord progressions; long skips in any voices are to be avoided, and indeed we should move largely step-wise, with occasional moderate skips. When the soprano moves over an arpeggio in repetitions of the same chord, the inner voices, and occasionally the bass, naturally skip, for that will be a musical leading of the voices.

To avoid any misconception, let us say that all exercises in this work begin and end on the tonic triad; a piece of music, however, frequently begins with some other chord, although the final chord will practically always be a tonic triad. (Two cases of an unusual beginning and ending are here given; they result from especial reasons. The first of these introduces a dramatic moment in the opera; while in the second one the dominant 7th chord ending the piece represents an expectation (a question, as the title indicates) which is answered in the piece immediately following. In ordinary music one has little to do with such things.)

" Tristan und Isolde," Introduction of Act II.

" Bittendes Kind" (from " Kinderscenen"; Schumann)

54. These examples from 1 to 31 are for four voices. Open and close position are to be used, and it is well to accustom one's self to change from one to the other in the same exercise; avoid an extended use of the extreme tones in any voice, keeping rather in the medium range; be careful in spacing the voices; always find and remember the 8ve and 5th in every chord, noticing also whether there be a leading-tone present.

In examples 1–7, the alto and tenor are to be added to the soprano and bass given. In ascertaining each chord count upward from the root, the other tones being the 3d and 5th; be careful to observe the rules given, as to consecutive 8ves and 5ths and the leading-tone, never allowing voices to cross each other.

WITH EACH CHORD CONSIDER THESE POINTS : 1. CAN WE TIE? SHALL WE TIE? 2. AVOID CONSECUTIVE 8VES AND 5THS. 3. IS THERE A LEADING TONE PRESENT? Only the roots of chords are given; be sure that the soprano begins on the right note.

NOTE. At × consider the succession V–VI; at ⤬ that of II–V; at ⤬ we have this point, that the repetition of a root often makes it desirable to get variety by the soprano (or, if not the soprano, the other voices) moving to another interval of the chord; 'n Ex. 19 we have a *sequence*, in which each voice must move with perfect regularity, measure by measure, *i.e.*, progress by the same intervals (the leading-tone being therefore doubled at one place).

55. Before harmonizing melodies it is necessary to say something with regard to the relative appropriateness of the triads for use with the different tones of the scale. Triads I, V, IV, and vi are the ones most used, ii and iii less often and vii° practically never, in root position, except in a sequence (see Ex. 19 preceding). Considering these triads singly, we shall find that in the major scale those indicated as follows under the different degrees are the ones most often employed, their relative frequency being also shown.

I	V	I	IV	V	IV	V
IV	ii	vi	ii	I	vi	
vi		iii	iii	iii	ii	iii

It is the custom to denote major triads by a large Roman numeral (I), minor triads by a small one (ii), augmented triads by a large one with a ⁺ after it, and diminished triads by a small one with a ° after it (III⁺, vii°); the augmented triad appears first with the minor scale. A ⁷ after a Roman numeral means a chord of the 7th (V ⁷, iii ⁷). In harmonizing melodies these signs will be much used to indicate the chords desired for particular notes; similarly major keys will be indicated by large letters (G), and minor keys by small ones (*e*).

CHAPTER V

HARMONIZING MELODIES IN MAJOR KEYS

56. We must also see what have proved to be the *best successions of triads in major keys*, although it is not possible to give more than an approximate idea of their relative frequency and importance. When a note is repeated in the soprano it is often well to change the triad; if a melody is built on the notes of a triad, it is likely that the bass will remain the same.

I   is followed by V, IV, **vi,** iii (seldom by ii).

ii "   "   "   V, **vi** ("   "   I, iii, IV).

iii "   "   "   vi, IV ("   "   ii, I, V).

IV "   "   "   V, I, ii ("   "   vi, iii).

V "   "   "   I, vi, iii, ii (sometimes by IV).

vi "   "   "   IV, iii, ii, V (seldom by I).

vii° need not be considered.

This table is applicable to triads only, not to inversions.

CHAPTER VI

TRIADS IN MINOR KEYS

57. As stated above (§ 27), every major scale has a minor scale so closely related to it (consisting of exactly the same tones with one exception) as to be called the Relative Minor. The tonic of this scale is always a minor third below the Relative Major, *e.g.* the scales of C major and *a* minor bear this relationship; in like manner G major and *e* minor, F major and *d* minor. *Relative Major and Minor Keys always have the same signature,* and the raising of the leading-tone is in every case to be indicated in the music itself; *e.g.* A♭ major and *f* minor would both have for a signature four flats, and E♮, the leading-tone of *f* minor, would have to be written, whenever it occurred.[1] The student is to write out for himself a table of signatures of all the major and minor keys, *e.g.*

Major Keys	Signature	Relative Minor Keys
C		*a* (G to be sharped)
G		*e* (D to be sharped), etc.

58. The triads erected on the successive degrees of the harmonic minor scale are as follows:

I   II°   III⁺   IV   V   VI   VII°

In classifying these triads we find that there are two minor triads, on the tonic and sub-dominant (I and IV); two major triads, on the dominant and the sixth degree (V and VI); two diminished triads, on the second degree and the leading-tone (II° and VII°), and one new and most distinctive triad, an *augmented* one on the third degree (III⁺). The minor scale is evidently richer in harmonic variety than the major, as it has three dissonant triads (II°, VII°, III⁺) as against one in major keys (the leading-tone triad).

---

[1] Capital letters (C) are used to designate major keys, and small letters in italics for minor keys (*a*).

59. A marked feature of the minor scale is the interval of an augmented 2d between the sixth degree and the leading-tone. Although this augmented 2d is often of great effect when used in a melodic way, it is generally better avoided in chord-progressions, especially in the inner voices. Much more latitude is allowed on this point in instrumental music than would be advisable in unaccompanied music for voices, for the augmented 2d is somewhat difficult to sing in tune.

60. In writing exercises in the minor mode the chief new points to be observed are these: First, the introduction and resolution of the three dissonant triads (II°, III⁺, VII°); Second, that no voice may *move* over the interval of an augmented 2d or 4th. The diminished triad (II°) may be connected with the triads VI and IV, and almost always resolves to the dominant.

We see now the importance of the recommendation as to the connection of II–V in the major mode (§ **48**); *i. e.* that the common tone is frequently not prolonged into the second chord ; the soprano, alto and tenor then proceeding in contrary motion to the bass (especially in close position). Observe the unvocal progression below of the augmented 2nd, and the good and vocal interval of the diminished 5th.

Observe that in the resolution of this dissonant triad the bass ascends a fourth. When dissonant chords of the seventh are treated, we shall see that the most natural resolution of all dissonances is for their bass to ascend a fourth (or, the same thing, to descend a fifth).

61. The augmented triad on the 3d degree (III⁺) is a harsh dissonance, and hence not commonly used in *root-position*, except where a striking effect is desired, *e.g.*

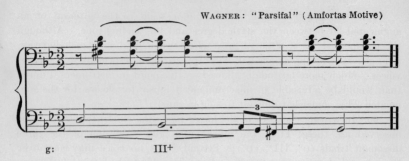

WAGNER: "Parsifal" (Amfortas Motive)

g: III+

When so used its resolution is generally to the triad on the sixth degree, *i.e.* the bass ascends a fourth, *e.g.*

III+ VI

but these resolutions are also good.

III+ II°   III+ IV

This mediant triad and, in fact, *all dissonant triads* (those with a diminished or an augmented 5th) are much more frequent and generally more effective as *chords of the 6th.* The augmented triad is very useful in this inversion to introduce dominant harmony, *e.g.*

III+ V₇

62. The diminished triad on the leading-tone in the minor mode (VII°), like the corresponding triad in major, is practically never employed; as a chord of the sixth, however, it is very useful and frequent. The bass is generally doubled, although at times the original fifth may be doubled with good effect, *e.g.*

(at (*a*) we see the bass doubled, and at (*b*) the original fifth).

63. When the dominant and sub-mediant triads (V and VI) are connected in the minor mode, the voices have to move along certain *fixed* lines in order to avoid consecutive 5ths and 8ves and the augmented 2d. The leading-tone always ascends to the tonic (or descends from it). Two of the upper voices must move in contrary motion to the bass, and the *3d is always to be doubled* in the triad on the sixth degree, *in four-part writing*.

When VI precedes V the same arrangement of voices is to be followed *e.g.*

64. *In a descending bass or soprano the melodic form of the minor scale is often used, i.e.* without the raised leading-tone (§ **22**). This is a survival of the old Aeolian Mode, which was identical with our scale of *a* minor with G, instead of G♯. The minor seventh, when so used, is generally harmonized with a chord of the 6th, *e.g.*

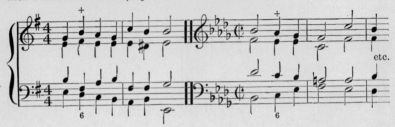

65. NOTE. It is not infrequently the case that a composition in a minor key is ended by a single chord in the tonic major. This major 3d in the final chord has been long known under the name of TIERCE DE PICARDIE (Picardy 3d); it was much used by Bach, and as a characteristic example the following is given, from his great G minor organ fugue :

it will be referred to later, in the chapter on modulation.

Before proceeding to the exercises that are to be written, there are given below two models; in analyzing them attention is drawn to these points, which must be considered in constructing every chord:

1. Are there tones that can be prolonged into the next chord ? If so, shall they be prolonged, or do we prefer to use contrary motion to the bass ?

2. If there are no tones that can be prolonged, in which direction shall the 8ve and 5th go ?

3. Is there a leading-tone in the chord ?

4. Is there an augmented interval to be avoided ?

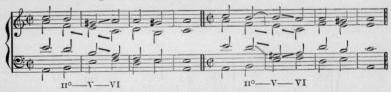

II°——V——VI   II°——V——VI

We have to avoid the interval of an augmented 2d (measures 1-2). In close position the soprano note is not tied; in open position it is, the tenor then supplying the necessary 3d in the following chord by making the good and vocal skip of a diminished 5th to G♯. Observe in each measure but the last the employment of contrary motion to the bass, to avoid consecutive 8ves and 5ths; also the progressions V–VI, and II°–V, and the choice of open and close positions in measures 3–4.

In Exercises 1–12 the bass is given; in 13–25 the bass is given, and a few chords of the 6th and 6-4 chords are introduced; in 20–25 the simple passing modulations of relative major and minor are introduced; and in 26–36 we have exercises for harmonizing melodies.

66. As the fact that we have one augmented triad, and the intervals of one augmented 2d and two augmented 4ths, affects the matter of triad-succession, for minor scales a table is given which differs from that for major ones:

I is often followed by V, VI, IV, II°, sometimes by III+ (when followed by II°, the 3d of I is usually in the soprano, the position being close).

II° is generally followed by V, occasionally by I, III+.

III+ " " " " VI, " " II°, IV (see examples in § 61).

IV " " " " V, I, II°.

V " " " " I, VI, III+, sometimes " IV.

VI " " " " IV, " " V, II°.

Note. The introduction of a few inversions (6th and 6-4 chords) will give more flexibility to our exercises. The student is referred for necessary information to the introductory paragraphs of the chapter on the Inversions of Triads. At present the bass of the chord of the 6th (the 3d of the original triad, cf. p. 20) is not to be doubled in any case; in 6-4 chords the bass should always be doubled. Until these chords are quickly recognized, their notes must be ascertained by counting upward from the bass the 3d and 6th, and 4th and 6th respectively.

Modulation is produced by means of a connecting succession of chords containing one or more tones foreign to the original key but belonging to the new one (e.g. in going from C major to a minor we introduce G♯, the leading-tone of a minor, while the change from a minor to C major is made by reversing the process, i.e. having G♮ in place of G♯). Our modulations here are passing ones, so much so as hardly to deserve the name, e.g.

67. It is advised that a few exercises with given bass be written for three voices. The basses of Nos. 1, 3, 6, 8, 10, 13, 14, 17, 18 (Chapter VII) are recommended. The following show how voices are doubled and omitted.

CHAPTER VII

TRIADS: EXERCISES IN MINOR KEYS

THE melody in the soprano should be made as varied and interesting as possible, and indeed good melodic movement in all the voices is desirable.

Write in all necessary accidentals.   Observe modulations in Nos. 20–25. At NB. *cf.* § 64.

23.

24.

25.

In harmonizing the following melodies, first ascertain the key (minor) of each exercise, and then the leading-tone, as well as the augmented skips that must be avoided. Chords of the 6th and 6-4 chords are indicated by those figures under the notes; Roman numerals show in particular cases the triads that should be used. Triads may sometimes be repeated; a triad may be followed by one of its inversions, and an inversion may often be followed by its triad; the leading-tone is always preceded by an accidental in minor keys.

26.

27.

28.

29.

30.

1-4; 1-5; 1-6; 2-5; 3-6; 4-2; 4-5; 5-3; 5-6; 6-2; 6-4; are common successions of triads in both major and minor keys; 1-6-4-5 and 1-6-4-2-5 are often used.

CHAPTER VIII

HIDDEN OCTAVES AND FIFTHS

68. WHEN two voices go in similar motion to a perfect 8ve or 5th, starting from some different interval, we have what is known as the progression of hidden 8ves or 5ths. One voice will necessarily move by skip, and sometimes both will do so.

From these illustrations we see the reason of the name; one voice passes over tones which, if sounded, would produce consecutive 8ves or 5ths; these 8ves and 5ths, being passed over and not sounded, are said to be hidden (or concealed).

Hidden unisons are less frequent, although they sometimes occur between tenor and bass,

or even between other voices (*cf.* § **70**).

69. N.B. *The student is strongly advised not to make a point of trying to avoid these hidden intervals. In the first place, questionable progressions of this sort will seldom occur if the chords are naturally connected in accordance with the given directions; and, secondly, a good melodic leading of the voices will justify all but a few cases.*

§ **70.** It may, however, be stated that hidden 8ves and 5ths are more noticeable, and often poor, when occurring in the outer voices; we shall not meet with the worst progression of this kind, that of a 7th or 9th followed by an 8ve, until we come to chords of the 7th.

A summary of the usual statements regarding these hidden intervals [1] is given on page 49; in the following examples, however, we see the futility of constructing rigid rules that are not really observed by musicians.

[1] Notice the hidden 8ves between outer parts in measure 1, and hidden 5ths between outer parts in measure 3 of each example; also the two hidden unisons.

NOTE. A condensation of the rules given in one of the most important manuals is as follows: Hidden 8ves are forbidden between soprano and bass except when (a) the bass rises a 4th (or falls a 5th) either from dominant to tonic, or tonic to sub-dominant, and at the same time the soprano moves by step; or (b) the second of the two chords is a 6-4 chord; or finally, (c) when the second chord is another position of the first. They are, however, allowed between any other two parts, excepting when a 7th or 9th moves to an 8ve in similar motion. Hidden 5ths between soprano and bass are forbidden except (a) in a progression from the tonic to the dominant chord, or from sub-dominant to tonic, in both of which cases the soprano must move by step of a second; (b) in a case like this;

and finally (c) from one to another position of the same chord. Hidden 5ths are not prohibited except between the outer parts.

CHAPTER IX

INVERSIONS OF TRIADS

Chords of the 6th, and 6-4 Chords

71. EVERY triad of a major or minor scale may appear in *inverted forms*, there being two inversions possible. To characterize these we employ the so-called *figured bass*, an old but excellent way of defining chords in speech and writing; musicians think and speak of chords by their figures. Words are saved, and there is a most satisfactory clearness;

for to say a chord of the 6th on D, and a 6-4 chord on F, is as plain as first inversion and second inversion respectively.

72. *In determining every chord, we in practice always count the intervals upward from the lowest tone. So in the following table, all the triads are composed of a root, 3d and 5th;* *he first inversions, of a bass (not root) 3d and 6th; the second inversions, of a bass (not root) 4th and 6th. These first and second inversions of triads are called "chords of the 6th" and "6-4 (six-four) chords."*

The inversions of triads on various degrees of the scale are useful in modulation, *e.g.*

Chords of the 6th and 6-4 chords must never be thought of as triads, but as inversions. It will be seen later that their treatment differs in important points from that used with triads. Unless this distinction is sharply made, the student is likely to become confused in his mind.

CHAPTER X

CHORD OF THE SIXTH

73. IT is impossible to make absolute rules with regard to the especial treatment of this chord, as exceptional cases are so numerous; there is nothing in harmony requiring more care, judgment, and good taste; but examples of the usual ways in which it appears will be given and analyzed, as well as some exceptions, a working scheme being deduced therefrom. What chiefly makes this chord difficult is that its bass is the 3d of the original triad, for it will be remembered that in triads that tone is comparatively seldom doubled. The question, therefore, as to doubling it becomes more complicated and difficult when the original 3d appears as the bass of the chord of the 6th, for we shall see that we can no longer usually double the bass, as we did with triads.

> *Reserve the term* ROOT *for the bass of the triad, and of chords of the 7th and 9th, thinking o* *the lowest tone of every inversion as its* BASS *simply; e.g. C is the* ROOT *of*

the BASSES *being E and G respectively.*

74. Now these chords appear in two ways, either singly or two or more in succession. Our decision on the above point as to doubling the bass will depend partly on mere sound, but even more on the melodic leading of the voices and the necessity of avoiding consecutive 8ves and 5ths and doubled leading-tones. In our discussion until § 76, the major scale is considered.

75. When the bass of a chord of the 6th is the tonic, the leading of the voices will determine as to the doubling.

When the bass is the second degree, the chord, being an inversion of the leading-tone triad,[1] naturally never doubles the leading-tone except in a sequence. (See Chapter XV.) We may then have these forms and others like them,

When the bass is the 3d of the scale, it is generally preferable to double one of the other tones, *inasmuch as the bass is the 3d of the tonic triad, and therefore of itself stands out conspicuously as the one tone determining the major or minor mode for the time being,*

although the melodic leading of the voices may result otherwise, *e.g.*

[1] It is in this inversion that the leading-tone triad is most useful, for we have seen that as a triad it is impracticable in most circumstances.

When the bass is the 4th of the scale, we are guided entirely by the leading of the voices

though it should be said that in minor scales this chord of the 6th is more euphonious if the bass be doubled, on account of the augmented fourth present, which is over-emphasized by the addition of another dissonance, the diminished 5th.

is a little better than

When the bass is the 5th of the scale, the leading of the voices will decide;[1]

when the 6th, it is rarely doubled when occurring singly ;

and finally, the bass on the 7th of the scale (leading-tone), should never be doubled.

[1] Notice the doubled leading-tone in (a); in chords of the 6th, the leading-tone, when not a root or 3d of the original triad, may sometimes be doubled, for in this connection it seems to lose its excessive prominence.

76. In minor scales the bass is seldom doubled when it is the tonic, often when on the 2d degree, often when on the 3d, usually when on the 4th, very often when on the 5th, often when on the 6th, never when on the 7th degree (leading-tone).

With both major and minor scales, if a chord of the 6th is the inversion of a *consonant* triad, the bass of the former will probably be doubled only in case better voice-leading results; if the original triad is *dissonant*, the bass of its inversion as a chord of the 6th is usually doubled.

CHAPTER XI

CHORDS OF THE 6TH IN SUCCESSION

77. Two or more successive chords of the 6th are often used, and we here note a marked difference between them and triads; for similar motion of all four parts, generally impossible with triads on account of the resulting consecutive 8ves and 5ths, is not uncommon with chords of the 6th.

Examples of the ordinary ways of so using these chords follow.

78. In (a) we must not double the bass of the second chord of the 6th, as consecutive 8ves would result between tenor and bass; but should double the bass in the third chord in order to avoid consecutive 8ves between soprano and tenor, and 5ths between alto and tenor, all the voices in this latter case being in similar motion: in (b) this similar motion is avoided by the use of open position. In (c) we have consecutive 5ths between alto and tenor, which are of perfectly good effect, one 5th being diminished. In (d) is shown a diatonic scale in the bass with consecutive chords of the 6th, in which example we notice a cardinal point — that a succession of these chords is often used *with the soprano a 6th above the bass and in similar motion with it, the alto also being in similar motion and the tenor moving alternately up and down. thus avoiding consecutive 8ves and 5ths;* it is of course seldom that so many of these chords appear in succession. The first chord of the 6th in (g) is used instead of a triad, so that there may be motion in one voice at least (the bass). In (h) and (i) we see that the melody in the soprano determines as to the doubling, while in (k) the bass of the first chord of the 6th is doubled to avoid consecutive 8ves and 5ths, although a different disposition of the voices would render this doubling unnecessary; in (l) we double to avoid having too many roots in the bass: in (m) and (o) the object is to have motion in some one voice, the melody in the soprano being stationary; in (p) is shown that *the bass is sometimes doubled in both chords, though not necessarily (soprano and bass being in contrary motion).*

79. It may happen that the parts become so arranged that the chord itself sounds poor, further leading of the voices also being difficult;

it is then better to change the soprano (consequently also the alto and tenor) thus:

Two mistakes often made by students are the following, to be avoided by changing the arrangement of voices in the first chord.

80. In going into the matter with such minuteness it is not expected or desired that the student shall memorize the examples, but rather use them for reference; there are, however, certain facts that may well be remembered, as summed up in the following

GENERAL DIRECTIONS.

1. While the bass of the chord of the 6th may be doubled upon any degree of the scale except 7 (leading-tone), this occurs most often on the 2nd degree, often on the 4th (especially in the minor scale) and on the 5th but less so on 1, 3 and 6.

2. When there are successive chords of the 6th, it is often the case that the soprano will proceed in similar motion with the bass and be a 6th above it; the other voices are to be so adjusted as to avoid consecutive 8ves and 5ths, and the bass will generally be doubled in every alternate chord (page 54, (*a*) (*b*) (*c*) (*d*)).

3. When there are successive chords of the 6th, and the soprano and bass are in contrary motion, the bass will often (but not always) be doubled in every chord.

4. The bass is frequently doubled simply to obtain a better melodic leading of the voices; in this case a good progression is to be preferred to a chord that sounds well, if there must be a choice.

CHAPTER XII

THE 6-4 CHORD

81. This chord is used in but few ways, and they can be definitely stated. In one respect it differs greatly from the chord of the 6th, in that we can safely say that its *bass is practically always doubled in four-part writing.* It is most often used on the accented part of the measure in the ordinary cadence forming the end of a composition or of a section of a composition, and in that case its bass is the dominant of whatever key we are in; the chord is followed by the dominant triad, this latter being often followed by the tonic triad of the same key. (See Chapter XIV.)

Sometimes a dominant 7th chord is used in this cadence.

NOTE. As the 6-4 chord, used in this way (accented), so often means a cadence, it very often appears as fixing a modulation,

although the expected modulation need not occur.

(2) It may be used (either on the accented or unaccented part of the measure), when preceded and followed by a triad having the same bass; although this is rather a weak progression, and chiefly employed for variety, to avoid having another triad, or a chord of the 6th.

(3) Also as a passing chord (c) and (d), in which case it is most likely to be unaccented.

Notice its strong cadential effect in (a), and that the chord is weak in (b) and (c), while in (d) the good result comes largely from the step-wise character of the bass.   In (c) we should do better to substitute a chord of the 6th.

(4) It may be used between a triad and a chord of the 6th of the same harmony.

82.   It is usually preceded in a cadence by a tonic, supertonic or sub-dominant triad (or the same as a chord of the 6th), sometimes by the sub-mediant.   e.g.

It is best to avoid having two 6-4 chords in succession, although this can be of good effect in some cases when the bass moves by step. Such a progression as this

is positively bad and ugly. In the following example, the second 6-4 chord is made to enter more naturally, chiefly through the diatonic movement of the bass.

In this — from the Third Organ Chorale of César Franck —

attention is called to the same diatonic movement of the bass, and also to the fact that the distinctive character of the 6-4 chord, as we chiefly meet with it, is negatived by the bass not being doubled on any one of the three chords.

NOTE. On page 8 of the score of Franck's D minor symphony, and at the entrance of the trombones in the second movement of Tschaikowski's 6th symphony, are instances of successive 6-4 chords; they are in these cases separated from each other by a single chord between, but the effect is none the less singular and worthy of note. For an illustration of these chords in succession with a diatonic bass, the student is referred to the seventh and eighth measures of the first movement of Mozart's C major symphony; and for a discussion of 6-4 chords on various degrees of the scale, the sixth chapter of Prout's "Harmony" should be consulted

---

CHAPTER XIII

EXERCISES WITH INVERSIONS OF TRIADS

83. REMEMBER that the following exercises are to be written without the help of any instrument; after writing, play them repeatedly, listening for characteristic points, and making changes after careful consideration. Play also the separate voice parts, to see whether the melodic progression can be improved. It is helpful to transpose exercises, and also to play them, reading from the bass alone; both of these things are at first difficult, but important aids towards clear musical thinking.

As we are now dealing with chords defined by figured basses, let us say that it is not enough simply to calculate the chords correctly in a mechanical way. Always try to obtain a varied melodic soprano and bass first of all, and then see how far the inner parts may be made interesting to sing and to hear. Monotony and stiffness are the worst faults; simple diatonic step-wise progression is preferable, skips being used with discretion. Bass notes without figures are, of course, the roots of triads.

RELATIVE MAJOR AND MINOR KEYS

84. In harmonizing melodies, it is to be remembered that especial attention must be given to the bass (§ **45**); we should try to have it melodious, preferring generally movement by step, rather than by skip, and avoiding awkward skips. An important gain resulting from the use of the chord of the 6th is that we can do away with pointless repetitions of the same bass tone, resulting from the repetition of a triad; in case the triad is repeated in root position, the bass may skip an 8ve, up or down, with good effect.

The skip of a 6th is unnecessary and not so natural as that of a 3d (measure 1 and **3-4**); skips of a 7th (measures 2, 3) are so awkward and unvocal that they must rarely be used; the monotonous repetitions in measures 4–5–6 can be improved by inversions; finally the 6 and 6-4 chords in measure 7 are excellent examples of what to avoid, each being weak and inappropriate in this connection.

Every note can form a part of three different triads (but *cf.* § 46), chords of the 6th and 6-4 chords; the one to be chosen, in each case, will depend on the chords just preceding and following. *E.G.* (Ex. 22).

In the following exercises, certain triads are indicated by Roman numerals; the 6 and 6-4 chords by those figures in most cases, though not always.

85. In three-part writing the 6 and 6-4 chords are to be complete, unless the leading of the voices is such that no ambiguity results from the omission of a tone (the chords marked ✕ are unmistakable.)

It is sometimes the case that an inner voice must move by a larger skip than when four voices are at our disposal; we may also find it desirable to have voices move over the intervals of a chord, to give a sense of completeness (as at ✕ ✕).

The basses of examples 1, 2, 3, 5, 6, 8, 10, 12, 13, are advised for three-part writing; in this the first rule on page 29 cannot be strictly observed.

CHAPTER XIV

CADENCES

86. THERE are four cadences in common use. The AUTHENTIC CADENCE is formed by the dominant triad (often with 7th added) followed by the tonic triad;

the strongest form of this being preceded by a 6-4 chord with the dominant for its bass; the soprano may end, in the final tonic triad, on either root, 3d or 5th.

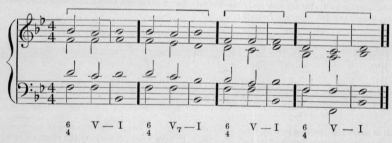

A few other forms follow, in which the dominant triad is introduced differently.

87. The PLAGAL CADENCE consists of the sub-dominant triad followed by tonic triad; the soprano ending on root, 3d or 5th.

IV — I   IV — I   IV — I

(Observe that the sub-dominant may appear as a 6-4 chord.)

This cadence is familiar in church music, being often used as an additional close after the Authentic Cadence:

V——I   IV——I

A beautiful example of Plagal Cadence in a major key, but with the sub-dominant triad a minor one, is in the very beginning of Mendelssohn's "Midsummer Night's Dream" Overture. Authentic and Plagal Cadences are called *Perfect* when the soprano ends on the tonic; when it is on the 3d or 5th, they are *Imperfect*.

88. The HALF CADENCE may in many cases be considered as a sort of reversal of the authentic:

I 6-4 — V

for it ends with the dominant triad, and is often preceded by the tonic in 6-4 position. It may, however, enter in other ways, *e.g.*

V   V

the usual definition of it being that it consists of any chord followed by the dominant triad. This cadence may be fitly compared with the semi-colon in punctuation, the authentic resembling the period; the half cadence leaves us in a state of suspense, for we feel that it does not mark an ending, but rather a pause, or interruption of the thought.   These two cadences, from their property of balancing each other, are complementary.   The deceptive cadence is not unlike a mark of interrogation (?).

NOTE.   Some theorists enlarge the possibilities of this cadence by admitting that its final chord may have other degrees of the scale (II, III, IV, VI) for its root.   In many cases such successions do have the especial effect of the half cadence, but the old custom was to restrict that name to such cadences as end with a dominant triad.   According to more recent opinion, however, all the passages in the following examples marked by a × would be considered to be half cadences.

WAGNER: "Tannhäuser" Overture

89. In the DECEPTIVE CADENCE the dominant triad, with or without a 7th (often preceded by the 6-4 chord, as in the authentic cadence), is followed by an unexpected chord, which leads us in some cases to a change of key.   A number of specimens are here given.

(The student is referred to the chapter on the dominant **7th for** further illustration.)

These cadences are sometimes named differently; but the terms Authentic and Plagal are well established, and Half Cadence and Deceptive Cadence express what is meant. While it is a question with the authentic cadence as to how far the use of a preceding 6-4 chord is needed, there is no doubt that the cadence is thereby strengthened.

CHAPTER XV

SEQUENCES

90. *A sequence is a regular and continuous change of position of a definite group of notes or chords, consisting of the group followed by at least two such transpositions.* According to its structure it will move, as a whole, either upwards or downwards,

and must progress without interruption in the same general direction, every interval being repeated in each voice identically, although the differences between major, minor, augmented, and diminished intervals are commonly disregarded. (This usual form of sequence (diatonic) is termed a *tonal* sequence; one in which the intervals retain their quality of major, minor, etc., is called *real, and is rarely used,* being indeed difficult to manage, and often impracticable, so far as concerns a good musical result.

As a sequence must be entirely regular, that quality in it is so important as to cause the minor prohibitions against doubled leading-tones and augmented skips to be disregarded.

91. Sequences are made much stronger, and **characteristic,** by an intermixture of dissonances (7th chords and their inversions).

It will be noticed in this last example that the dissonances (marked ×), forming an integral part of it, make the sequence *inevitable*, until it is finally given up in the seventh measure; for each dissonance, having its necessary, and, in every case, similar resolution, forces us to perfect regularity. The sequence is a device easily abused, and care must be taken to introduce it only where it really adds to musical strength and interest.

It affords a convenient, pliable, and attractive means of modulation, by the possible chromatic changes in various tones. In the last illustration an E♯ introduced in the fourth measure would lead to f♯ minor, a G♮ in the same measure perhaps to b minor, a D♯ in the sixth measure to E major.

92. Reference should be made to the figure called *Rosalia.* This is practically the same as a sequence, the name being derived from an old Italian popular song, "Rosalia, mia cara," the melody of which is constructed by repeating a figure several times in succession, and transposing it a tone higher at each reiteration; the figure usually appears not more than three times in succession (*cf*. Schumann, "Arabeske," op. 18).

93. From this time on, the student is advised to write at least some of the exercises on four staves, for the present being restricted to the two clefs thus far used. In the clef of the tenor voice it is understood that the tones are an 8ve lower than those indicated by the notes.

will be written

It will be well to begin by taking some of the exercises that have been previously written on two staves, and to rewrite them on four staves; writing entirely on four staves after a little of this preliminary experience.

The introduction of especial clefs for alto and tenor (the C-clefs) will be made later.

CHAPTER XVI

CHORDS OF THE SEVENTH

94. By adding to any triad the tone a seventh above its root (§ **30**), we obtain a chord of the 7th; and, as there are seven triads in every major and minor scale, we have seven chords of the 7th in every scale. They differ from triads and their inversions in being all *dissonant chords,* varying in degree of harshness, by reason of the specific kind of their 5ths and 7ths.

95. Being dissonant they demand some sort of resolution in nearly all cases, although it will be seen later that it is possible to have the voices so progress that, properly speaking, there is no resolution at all.

RESOLUTION must now be defined: *by that term is understood the chord following the 7th chord; this chord of resolution may be consonant or dissonant.* a full account of its possibilities being given later under the heading of Irregular Resolutions. Of these 7th chords, those founded upon the dominant (V) and leading-tone (VII°) have a less pronounced dissonant quality than the others, and may enter in all circumstances without preparation, *i.e.* without the necessity of either root or 7th being a prolongation of a tone in the preceding chord (*cf.* chapter on secondary sevenths). As the one of which the dominant is the root is far more used than any of the others, our first attention will be devoted to it.

THE DOMINANT SEVENTH CHORD

96. This chord is composed of a root, major 3d, perfect 5th, and minor 7th, and has especial characteristics: (1) *that it is the same for major and minor tonic keys;* (2) *that it is the only chord so far discussed that of itself defines the key* [1] *(though not the mode);*

and (3) *that it is therefore much used in the authentic cadence* (§ 86).

[1] No triad (or its inversion) defines a key by itself, the feeling of tonality coming from a succession of them;

can be I in C major, IV in G major, V in F major or *f* minor, VI in *e* minor (and even III in *a* minor when form (*f*) of the minor scale is used, § 22). But with

the note F♮ shows that there is no sharp in the signature, the B♮ that there can be no flat, and the G♮ that we cannot be in *a* minor, so that the chord must belong to either C major or *c* minor. It should be stated that in a minor key the accidental chromatically raising the 3d of the chord of the 7th is always written each time that it occurs. as we have also found to be the case with triads and their inversions.

leading tone different from 7th of a chord

97. While there are various irregular resolutions of the dominant 7th, we find such a preponderance of cases in which musical habit and feeling demand that the *7th descend one degree* as to be justified in laying that down as its ordinary resolution.

The *leading-tone* (forming the 3d of the chord) when present, *usually ascends to the tonic;*[1] sometimes, when in an inner voice, it descends to the 5th of the chord of resolution, to supply that desirable interval, which would otherwise be lacking.

It is preferable, in this latter case, to have the bass in contrary motion to the leading-tone and the 7th, as the progression of the voices is thus made more symmetrical.

And since through this resolution of the 7th and 3d, we obtain two tones of the tonic triad, it is most natural for the root of the 7th (ascending a 4th or descending a 5th) to go also to the root of that triad. The *5th* (when present, it being often omitted) *will naturally descend to the tonic,* although it sometimes ascends one degree for melodic reasons.

98. The root is frequently doubled, the 5th being then the tone usually omitted, the 3d less often. This doubled root, whether in soprano, alto, or tenor, must be nearly always continued in the same voice in the chord of resolution.

[1] Two tones forming a diminished interval have a tendency to converge; those forming an augmented interval to diverge.

There are cases, when we should
naturally double the root,

where we may lead the soprano
thus, for melodic reasons

The 3d (leading-tone) and the 7th, *sensitive tones*, stand out so prominently that neither of them may be doubled. It is also preferable not to double

[1] This point is not so obvious as that concerning the prohibition of consecutive 8ves. The result (*a*) of a 7th or 9th *moving* to an 8ve is bad, as is also (*b*) that of an 8ve moving to a 7th or 9th, (*c*) of a unison moving to a 2nd, or a 2nd to a unison, or (*d*) a unison moving to a 7th.

As similar motion towards a dissonance is often undesirable, it is better to change the disposition of the voices in (*a*) to that given in (*b*).

the 5th, as both chords would then have one tone missing, thereby producing a thin and poor effect.

99. Be careful about consecutive 5ths; the strong character of the 7th so easily obscures the sound of the 5th, that especial attention must be paid to this point.

It is usually the case that one of the two chords, either that of the 7th or of its resolution, will be incomplete.

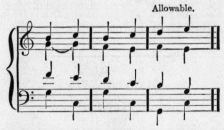

It is allowable to have all four voices progress in similar motion.

100. Here is a statement of the ordinary resolution of this chord:

1. THE 7TH REGULARLY DESCENDS ONE DEGREE.
2. THE 3D (LEADING-TONE), WHEN PRESENT, USUALLY ASCENDS TO

THE TONIC; SOMETIMES, WHEN IN AN INNER VOICE, DESCENDING TO THE 5TH OF THE FOLLOWING TRIAD. *(descends 2 degrees)*

3. THE 5TH, WHEN PRESENT, USUALLY DESCENDS TO THE TONIC. *Can ascend 1d*

4. THE ROOT, WHEN IN THE BASS, MOVES TO THE TONIC; WHEN IN ANOTHER VOICE ALSO, IT IS PROLONGED IN THAT VOICE INTO THE NEXT CHORD.

ENTRANCE OF THE DOMINANT 7TH CHORD

101. The seventh may (*a*) be a prolongation of a tone from the preceding chord, (*b*) enter by step, (*c*) enter by skip.

Although the regular treatment of this chord is somewhat inflexible, we yet have now obtained some more material for our work, and shall find greater variety and interest in it. The exercises appropriate to this subject wiii be found in Chapter XVIII. OBSERVE THE CONSECUTIVE 5THS (BUT ONE OF THEM BEING PERFECT) IN (*b*). *Cf.* pp. 55, 107. For dominant 7ths in cadences, see p. 66. The dominant 7th is frequently preceded by the dominant triad without the 7th.

CHAPTER XVII

PASSING AND AUXILIARY TONES

102. WE shall gain greatly in our voice parts by the introduction of occasional Passing and Auxiliary Tones. Even in exercises it is desirable to write musically and melodically without stiffness; as is the case in actual composition, these non-harmonic tones interposed between the harmonic tones of chords will prove our best aid toward attaining that object.

It is a familiar statement that melody is horizontal (moving, as it were, in a line ——) *and that chords are vertical (||||).*

BEETHOVEN: 9th Symphony

etc

TSCHAIKOWSKI: 6th Symphony

SCHUMANN: Soldatenmarsch, Op. 68

When non-harmonic tones of any sort are introduced in any voice, the melody thus produced becomes naturally more independent as regards the chords through which it moves, and we have a beginning of contrapuntal treatment of such a voice. Observe the square-cut, ponderous effect of the following (*a*), and the free, flowing melodic line of the separate voices in (*b*).

"Ein' Feste Burg"
AUGUST HAUPT: Choralbuch

HASSLER: Passion Chorale

PASSING TONES

103. By this term is meant non-harmonic tones that are interposed in any voice between harmonic tones of two successive chords; they may be either (*a*) diatonic or (*b*) chromatic, and may occur in any one of the four voices.

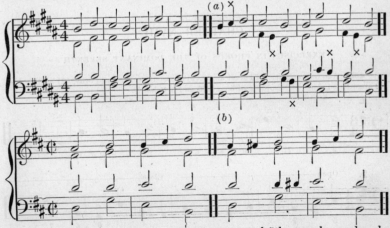

No skips are allowed, and no consecutive 8ves and 5ths may be produced.

AUXILIARY TONES

104. An auxiliary tone is a non-harmonic tone which returns to that tone from which it started, and moves at the distance of a tone or semitone above or below: it will be of course, as is the passing tone, dissonant from at least a part of the chord with which it is sounded. Consecutive 8ves and 5ths must be looked out for.

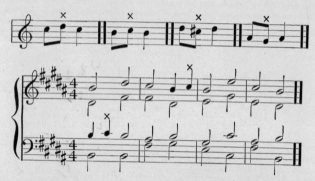

It is not intended that the student shall try to introduce either passing or auxiliary tones excepting in a natural way and for the improvement of the melody; in many cases there will be successions of chords where such tones are inappropriate, or even incorrect. And it is advisable, before using these ornamental tones in the exercises that follow, to go back to the simpler exercises in triads and their inversions, rewriting a few of them in this manner.

CHAPTER XVIII

EXERCISES IN CHORDS OF THE DOMINANT SEVENTH

105. ALL former rules hold good as to (1) consecutive 8ves and 5ths, (2) leading-tone, (3) augmented skips, (4) doubling of bass in 6 and 6-4 chords.

In some of the following exercises is introduced an irregular resolution of the dominant 7th chord, to a triad on the 6th degree. This progression is very common indeed; the *tendency tones* (the 7th and leading-tone) have the same resolution as regularly, the only difference being that the root does not go to the tonic triad. Much of the stiffness that would otherwise be felt is done away with by employing this resolution.

The chord of the 7th is usually complete (p. 74).

Observe that in Ex. 4, 6, 11, 17, 19, we do not have groups of 4 and 8 measures, but those of 6; in Ex. 13, 16, we have groups of 3, with 3-measure rhythm.

Before writing the following exercises for three voices, refer to the directions for similar ones at the close of the chapters on Inversion of Triads: it is only necessary to add here that the root and 7th in the chord must of course be always present, and that it is quite a matter of choice whether the 3d or 5th be the interval omitted. We may indeed introduce both of them, by employing this device.

We may also choose between these two.

A model of three-part writing with dominant 7ths.

(Observe that the incomplete 6 and 6-4 chords are not at all doubtful; a passing tone is used in measure 3, and an auxiliary tone in measure 4.)
Exercises for three voices.

Exercises in harmonizing a melody for four voices.

Dominant 7th chords are indicated by V⁷; when a Roman numeral without a 7 is used, it means either a triad or its inversion, the root being the degree given (I, vi, etc.).

In the following exercises for four voices no figures are given: in nearly every chord there is a choice to be made, e.g. of a triad or chord of the 6th, a triad or 6-4 chord, a triad or chord of the 7th.

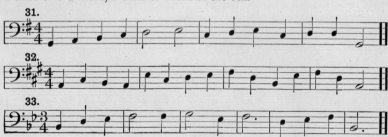

CHAPTER XIX

INVERSIONS OF THE DOMINANT 7TH CHORD

106. By inverting this chord, we obtain the following:

and to designate them clearly, count upward, as usual, from the bass. *As the root and 7th of the original chord are the two characteristic tones that define it, these same two tones are selected in naming the particular inversion employed.* That is (with the chords given above) C and B flat are 1 and 7 of the dominant 7th chord, and 6 and 5 of the first inversion, 4 and 3 of the second inversion, and 2 and 1 of the third inversion. We therefore naturally always speak of the 6-5 and 4-3 chords, and of chords of the 2d (the last one also as the 4-2 chord). After counting the intervals upward from the bass, *refer back in thought to the original chord of the 7th;* this is necessary in order to be sure as to which tone is the root and which the 7th. In minor keys the 3d of the 7th chord will of course be chromatically raised in the inversions as well.

107. THE REGULAR RESOLUTION *of the 7th* in these inversions is the same as with the original chord, *i.e. it descends one degree; the root, being in every case in a voice not the bass, is prolonged into the following chord in the same voice; the leading tone (3d) will ascend to the tonic; the 5th may go to any tone of the chord following.*

The 7th may be prolonged from the preceding chord, or may enter by step or by skip.

Two consecutive 5ths may be used, if one of them is not perfect (pp. 106-108). With inversions of V7 it is usual to have the chord complete.

CHAPTER XX

SOME SIMPLE MODULATIONS

108. ANOTHER way of making our exercises more helpful and musical is afforded by the introduction of a few of the most usual modulations (§ 66). As we have enriched our material by the addition of the dominant 7th and of its inversions, so much employed in the authentic cadence and in modulation, it is right that we should now learn something of their practical use in that respect. For the present we restrict ourselves to the modulations between a major tonic key and its relative minor (VI), dominant (V), and sub-dominant (IV).

A modulation is effected by introducing one or more tones found in the key to which we are going and not in that which we leave; it is usually first indicated by the presence of the leading-tone of the new key, and is often definitely fixed by an authentic cadence,[1] the latter sometimes including a 6-4 chord.

109. In going from A major to its dominant, we first introduce the leading-tone of the new key, E major, and confirm the modulation with an authentic cadence (with or without the 7th). In going from F major to its sub-dominant, we lower the leading-tone a semitone (by the introduction of (E♭) thus having a new leading-tone (A) of the new key, B flat major, and concluding with an authentic cadence. In going from E♭ major to its relative minor we introduce the leading tone (B♮) of the new key, and fix the modulation by an authentic cadence.

---

[1] The mere presence of the leading-tone of another key does not of itself mean a modulation, as it may simply indicate a chromatically changed chord.

A modulation from V to I is the same as I to IV, and from IV to I the same as I to V.   The modulation from a minor key to its relative major is made by cancelling the leading-tone of the minor, in which case we of course have for a new leading-tone that of the new key.

Mark the entrance of the new key in each case (writing, *e.g.* D for D major, *g* for *g* minor); introduce a few passing and auxiliary tones.

Before writing our next exercises, it is necessary to say this about the progression V⁷–vi (V⁷–VI in minor keys) — that for the present it is to be used in root-position alone, and that it must be complete, *i.e.* the root must not be doubled (§ 105).

CHAPTER XXI

110. EXERCISES with dominant 7ths and their inversions; the inversions always resolve regularly, and the chords of the 7th likewise (with the exception of occasional V⁷–vi, V⁷–VI).

12.

13.

14. Open————————————Close

15.

16.

17. Open—————————Close.

18. (Chant)

19.

Model of three-part writing: inversions of dominant 7ths.

Passing tones in measures 2, 4–5, 5–6, 8, 9: auxiliary tones in measures 1, 3, 7: in measures 7, 8, the complete chords are obtained by a voice moving over two tones of the chord, an excellent resource in many cases.

The two upper voices will necessarily be in some cases at a greater distance from the bass than would be advisable in four-part writing; in every chord of the 7th (or inversion) the root and 7th must be present; use a few passing tones .

23. (Examples 23–32 are for three voices.)

Melodies to be harmonized for four voices. V⁷ signifies either a dominant
7th chord or one of its three inversions; our choice will be determined by
the chord-succession, *i.e.*, by considering the chords preceding and following.

for a good melodic bass must be obtained. By a Roman numeral (I, II) is understood either the triad or one of its two inversions. Dominant 7ths or their inversions are to be used at various places not indicated.

In nearly every measure of the following bass melodies to be harmonized for four voices, there are dominant 7ths, or inversions of the same.

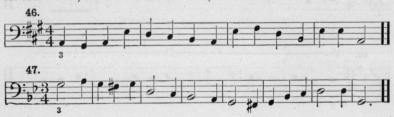

In the above observe how natural the successions V–V⁷ and IV–V⁷
are (see p. 104 also).

CHAPTER XXII

IRREGULAR RESOLUTIONS OF THE DOMINANT 7TH

111. CONDITIONS arising from the melodic leading of the voices, or
from the chord following the dominant 7th chord, frequently bring about
very different resolutions from the regular one; for the 7th in that chord
(*a*) may be prolonged in the same voice into the next chord, (*b*) may ascend, or (*c*) may even give up its resolution, for the time or definitively.

The root may (*a*) be prolonged into the next chord, (*b*) ascend **or descend** to an interval other than the regular one. Illustrations of these latter points may be found in §116.

112. The 7th may be continued as a diatonic tone into the next chord:

or as an enharmonically changed tone, a sudden modulation resulting.

113. It may be resolved upward (*cf.* §120, 146) by step diatonically (in which case its resolution occurs in another voice) (*a*), chromatically (*c*), or by skip (*d*); (*a*) being much used when I or i, as a chord of the 6th, follows V⁷ (*cf.* as to the 5ths §120); (*b*) is very bad (p. 74). It also sometimes descends by skip (*e*).

114. The dominant 7th chord sometimes abandons its resolution altogether, being followed by chords that obliterate the impression which it has made *as a chord of the 7th*:

or does so for a moment, but returns and completes the expected resolution:

or transfers the 7th to another voice in the next chord, the resolution being made in the latter voice.

It may also transfer its 7th to another voice in an inversion of itself; in fact several inversions may be used in succession (as is the case with triads and their inversions).

Another tone of the same chord (8ve, 5th or 3d) may be interposed between the 7th and its resolution.

115. A dominant 7th chord in either a major or minor key may progress to any triad of its own key (except VII°).

The succession V⁷–VI, being a very common one, was spoken of in § 105, and has already been used in our exercises (as also V⁷–VI in minor keys).

It is sometimes stated that the dominant 7th chord may progress to any 7th chord in its own key; not all of these successions, however, are of real value.

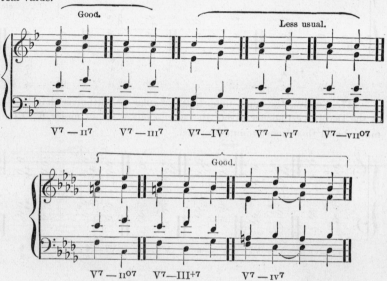

116. It may be resolved into a dominant 7th chord of another key (or its inversion); most often into one belonging to one of the five nearest related keys.

It may be resolved into the diminished 7th chord (or one of its inversions) of another key.

117. Finally, the most important irregular resolution is that known as the Deceptive Cadence (§ **89**), the successions V⁷-vi in major, V⁷-VI in minor being those most commonly used.

Observe that in many deceptive cadences of which the dominant 7th forms a part, that chord must be complete; for if the root be doubled it will usually be the case that one of the voices will fail to have a good progression.

In (*a*) the alto would make consecutive 8ves with the bass if it ascended to A, and we should have a second followed by a unison in similar motion (§ 98) if it went to E; it may, to be sure, cross the tenor and descend to C, but this is not to be recommended. It is better to change the first chord, thus:

A similar explanation will suggest itself to the student as regards (b); and it is advised that (b) be rewritten, changing the first chord, so that each voice may have a musical and natural progression.

NOTE. We sometimes have occasion to use a chord looking like a dominant 7th (being composed of a root, major 3d, perfect 5th, and minor 7th), which occurs through a chromatic change really not affecting the key in which we are (§ 109); an apparent dominant 7th, in this case looking like an inversion, may also result from the introduction of a passing tone.

All of the above is intended for a statement and for reference, but is not to be committed to memory. Every example recommended may be found illustrated in the best music, and the student will find out by practical work which of these resolutions are of general use, for some of them are seldom employed. The dominant 7th, with its various irregular resolutions, is a most flexible chord.

CHAPTER XXIII

118. EXERCISES: IRREGULAR RESOLUTIONS OF THE DOMINANT 7TH

9. (Observe the so-called feminine ending of this example.)

18.

MELODIES TO BE HARMONIZED

As before, V⁷ means either a dominant 7th chord or one of its inversions; a Roman numeral (V, III, III$^\times$, VII°) means a triad or one of its inversions.

In each of these bass melodies there are to be both regular and irregular resolutions (*cf.* p. 93).

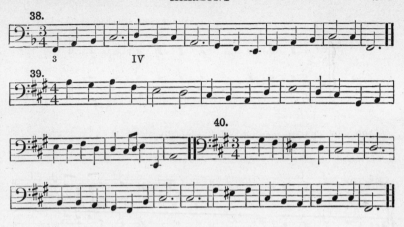

CHAPTER XXIV

IRREGULAR RESOLUTIONS OF INVERSIONS OF THE DOMINANT SEVENTH

119. (1) THE 7th may be prolonged into the next chord.

1 As with triads and their inversions, dominant 7th chords and their inversions are interchangeable one with another; the last 7th chord or inversion that appears must of course be finally resolved. (The case is similar with the other 7th chords, and with augmented 6th chords, etc.), e. g.

BEETHOVEN: 7th Symphony

120. (2) The 7th may ascend diatonically.

In (*a*) the 7th in the alto ascends, abandoning its resolution to the bass, as it is not desirable here to double the bass of the ensuing chord of the 6th; in (*b*) a useful fact again appears (see the note on p. 55) — that *two consecutive 5ths are admissible, in case one of them is not perfect (i.e. is either diminished or augmented).*

NOTE.   If

is played, the effect is musical and entirely satisfactory, so far as sound is concerned. If the above consecutive 5ths be changed so that all are perfect, the passage cannot be made endurable, for there is no disposition of the other voices possible that will sufficiently obscure or soften the 5ths.

121. (3) The 7th may ascend chromatically.

This last succession might also appear in the following manner, the soprano being written in both ways, and the modulation thus definitely shown.

122. (4) The inversions may resolve to dominant 7th chords (or their inversions) in other keys, or to diminished 7th chords, or their inversions (Chapter XXVIII).

(*Observe the consecutive diminished 5ths in the above.*)

As regards these successions of 5ths, where they are not all perfect ones and we do not class them as consecutive 5ths (§ **43**), there have been various rules made. But, as is usually the case in music, it is really the question of what sounds well that should decide for theorists.

as well as for composers. We find that the progressions of a perfect 5th followed by a
diminished one, and of a diminished 5th followed by a perfect one, practically always occur
when the 4-3 chord of the dominant 7th and the chord of the 6th of the tonic triad are employed, as above. The progression is less pure when other degrees of the scale are used; in
the following it is better, *e.g.* to omit the 5th in the chord of the 7th (if the key were major, we
should of course have consecutive 5ths).

123. Successive diminished 5ths (in diminished 7th chords) may occur
moving upward or downward, moving by diatonic or chromatic step, or by
skip, and to any extent. This is, however, a progression easily abused,
for the ear quickly gets tired of the sound; like any pronounced flavor, a
little of it will go a long way.

There are cases when a perfect 5th may be followed by an augmented one,
or an augmented 5th by a perfect one, *e.g.*

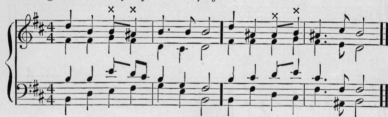

124. The progressions V⁷-vi, V⁷-VI are commonly used with the
chords in root position;

with the 6–5 chord we can get a satisfactory progression in minor keys, but in major keys the result is poor;

the following (4–3 chord) is not recommended; a better progression for obtaining the result desired can always be found;

the chord of the 2d chiefly occurs when the bass is moving diatonically, for such a melodious and symmetrical leading of the voices is here, as often, the means by which a smooth and logical progression is obtained.

CHAPTER XXV

125. IRREGULAR RESOLUTIONS OF DOMINANT 7TH CHORDS AND OF THEIR INVERSIONS.

Melodies to be harmonized. (V⁷ has the same significance as in previous exercises. The harmonies indicated are to be regarded as merely suggestive.)

18.

IV V⁷   V⁷   VI

In *g*————————In *d*.

19.

III   V IV V⁷   I

In F————————————————————In *d*————

V⁷ V⁷ In F.   III   VI

In F.   In B flat.

20.

5   V⁷ In *g*.   IV

In *c*.   III⁺

Bass melodies to be harmonized with regular and irregular resolutions of dominant 7ths and their inversions.

21.

6   4   6   7
4   2   5   ♯

22.

6   IV   7 6 7
4   4

23.

3   6   IV I
      5

24.   Open.

3   IV

CHAPTER XXVI

CHORDS OF THE SEVENTH ON THE LEADING-TONE

I. In Major Keys

126. Chords of the 7th of which the leading-tone is the root are like dominant 7th chords in differing from the others (I^7, II^7, III^7, IV^7, VI^7) through their relatively more frequent use without preparation (Chapter XXX); the same is true of their inversions. We first take up the leading-tone 7th chord in major keys.

127. It may enter by a prolongation of its 7th from the preceding chord, by step or by skip.

The regular resolution is for its 7th to descend one diatonic tone, its root to ascend to the tonic, its 5th to descend one diatonic tone, and its 3d to ascend or descend according to circumstances.[1]

[1] NOTE. As in every chord of the 7th, there are two 5ths, when the soprano has the 7th,

we see in the following the likelihood that in some cases consecutive 5ths may be carelessly written; these can be avoided by having (a) the tenor or alto ascend (doubling the 3d of the ensuing triad), or by letting the tenor skip (making perfectly good hidden 8ves with the soprano). In (c) the soprano does not have the 7th, but we have a similar case, treated in the same manner.

128. The 7th may fail to resolve, being prolonged in the same voice into the next chord.

Observe that, while the first chord marked ✕ is really a leading-tone 7th, from its relation to the preceding chord, the second one so marked has lost that character, for we are at that point modulating to the relative minor.

129. Although the root, being leading-tone, has, of course, a strong tendency to ascend to the tonic, it sometimes ascends to another degree.

130. But one of the inversions of this chord is in common use, as a real leading-tone 7th.

The others may be used as passing chords, but in this way largely lose their character as leading-tone 7ths.

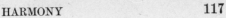

No interval of this chord, or of its inversions, may be omitted or doubled.

CHAPTER XXVII

EXERCISES WITH THE LEADING TONE 7TH

(The × signifies that the 7th of the chord is to be placed in the soprano.)

131.

Melodies to be harmonized.   Leading-tone 7ths are indicated by the ×.

Bass melodies to be harmonized, with at least one 7th chord on the leading-tone (or inversion) in every exercise. Observe the passing tones (indicated by slur ⌢).

CHAPTER XXVIII

CHORDS OF THE SEVENTH ON THE LEADING–TONE

II. *In Minor Keys*

THE CHORDS OF THE DIMINISHED SEVENTH

132. IN minor keys the 7th of the leading-tone chord of the 7th is a diminished one, the chord being consequently known as the *diminished seventh chord.*

In major keys the 7th of the leading-tone 7th is sometimes chromatically lowered a semitone, so that we may have a diminished 7th chord in such keys also.

It may also similarly be the case that a passage in a minor key ends with a major triad

The 7th may enter (*a*) as a prolongation from the preceding chord, (*b*) step-wise, or (*c*) by skip.

The 7th may be resolved (*a*) one diatonic semitone downward, (*b*) be prolonged into the next chord, or (*c*) occasionally ascend. The root (*a*) usually moves upward to the tonic, but (*b*) may be prolonged into the next chord, or (*c*) even progress downward (in which latter case there is often a modulation).

It will be observed that when the chord of resolution is a triad, the 3d or 5th is often doubled, as is also the case (§ 127) with leading-tone 7th chords in major keys.

MOZART: "Ave verum"

133. It is permissible to have the interval of an augmented 2d in the following chord-progression; the reason is probably that the leading-tone being present (and therefore conspicuous) in each chord, makes that interval vocally more natural; the alternative to this is obviously similar motion in all four parts.

134. All of the inversions are useful. No tone may be omitted or doubled in either the original chord of the 7th or any of its inversions.

135. The chord of the diminished 7th is the most ambiguous of all chords, forming a strong contrast to the dominant 7th chord in this respect. As with our tempered scale, we get practically the same sound effect from diminished 7th chords with different notations (and, therefore, belonging to different keys),[1] we must be careful how we write them. In determining the key to which such a chord belongs, always look for the leading-tone, *e.g.*

a   c   e flat   f sharp

To find the key in the first of these, we ascertain that there can be no sharp or flat in the signature; the key is therefore C major or *a* minor, and the leading-tone, G sharp, determines that the latter is the case.

The student is to find the keys to which the following chords belong:

There naturally are diminished 7th chords on every degree of the chromatic scale; they may be written in different ways enharmonically, as is seen above. Any dominant 7th chord can be made into a diminished 7th chord by raising its root chromatically.

CONSECUTIVE CHORDS OF THE DIMINISHED SEVENTH

136. Such successions often occur; the following examples will repay study:

BACH: Chromatic Fantasie

BEETHOVEN: Sonata, Op. 10, No. 3

etc.

[1] This chord, therefore, furnishes an easy and effective means of modulation; too obvious, indeed, for it has been used with such frequency, both in and out of season, that the freshness which it once had has now been pretty well lost. In Spohr we have a conspicuous instance of a composer whose work was weakened by the excessive use of diminished 7ths.

137. A diminished 7th chord or one of its inversions may, in some circumstances, be preceded or followed (a) by the same or another diminished 7th chord or one of its inversions, (b) by a dominant 7th chord or one of its inversions, or (c) by a secondary chord of the 7th chord, or one of its inversions (the secondary 7th chords very rarely in root position).

138. The diminished 7th chord is sometimes approached in modulation in such a way that a so-called *cross-relation* is made; this, however, is of good effect, provided that there is a good leading of the voices (*cf.* Ex. 2, 6, in Chapter XXIX).

CHAPTER XXIX

139. EXERCISES WITH CHORDS OF THE DIMINISHED 7TH

3.

4.

5.

Passing tones are indicated by the slur ⌢.

6.

7. (Chant)

8.

9.

Melodies to be harmonized; diminished 7th chords and their inversions are indicated by the ×. Write these exercises on four staves; introduce a few passing tones.

Bass melodies to be harmonized with occasional diminished 7th chords and their inversions. Passing tones are indicated by slurs.

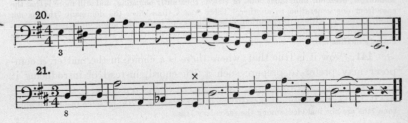

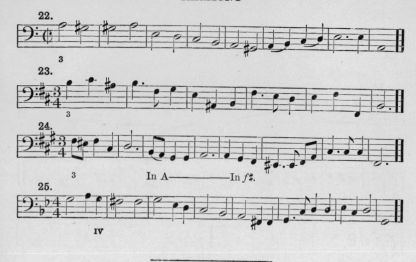

In A————In f♯.

CHAPTER XXX.

SECONDARY CHORDS OF THE SEVENTH

140. ALL chords of the 7th, whose roots are on other degrees of the scale than the dominant, have been generally classed as secondary (or collateral) 7ths; they were formerly, with the exception of the leading-tone 7th,[1] considered to be subject to a rigid rule as regards their entrance (the so-called *preparation*), this rule holding good with their inversions also.

The strict observance of this academic rule has for a long time been disregarded by composers; it should be remembered that rules of harmony worthy of observance have been gradually deduced, during the evolution of modern music, from what has been actually written. The music does not spring from the rules, but the really important laws (better that word than rules) ever remain to guide us, though modified from time to time to meet the requirements of later developments.

It is true that in music, as in other things, the radical of to-day is the conservative of to-morrow; even our individual point of view is constantly changing, and still more is that the case from one generation to another. There was a time when the dominant 7th was not allowed to enter without preparation; other changes of feeling are going on in our own time, for we have seen *e.g.* during the last fifty years the old doctrine about cross-relations become entirely modified.

141. Now it is true that, where there is a choice in the matter, a composer may prefer to prepare such a 7th chord, instead of introducing it

---

[1] It is because the leading-tone 7th is understood by all theorists to require no preparation that it has been discussed immediately after the dominant 7th; by some theorists leading-tone 7ths are not included among the secondary 7ths.

freely, — it is also the case that the chord progression is often such that it is necessary to have the preparation, as otherwise the leading of the voices would be awkward, or result in harshness. The point to emphasize is simply this, that by reasonable theorists and musicians this rule as to preparation is no longer considered absolute, nor of sufficient consequence to stand against a better way of producing the result desired, if that way preclude the preparation of the 7th chord. The course to be taken will, in every case, depend on the judgment of the composer; a few hints, however, will not be out of place, even though no really definite statement can be made.

The following is given as an example of an unprepared 7th, where the chord of the 7th is of itself less harsh, having the interval of a minor 7th.

It is, indeed, difficult to see why the secondary 7th chords II^7, III^7, VI^7 (in major) should be considered essentially much harsher than the dominant and leading-tone 7ths.

It is clear from the above (a) that the 7th (when without preparation) enters best in a 6-5 chord; (b) that contrary motion between root and 7th softens the harshness; (c) that the 7th enters best step-wise. The 4-3 chord and the chord of the 2d are not easy to introduce well without preparation.

The statements given later as to the resolutions of these 7th chords hold good, whether the chords be prepared or not.

NOTE. "Even in the last century the old law as to the preparation and progression of these chords was often disregarded; and it would be absurd to fetter ourselves now by any such rule. *Any essential discord may be taken without preparation.*" (From Prout's "Harmony.")

142. To illustrate the unrestricted way in which 7ths may be used in free contrapuntal writing this example is given; some of the 7ths being passing-tones or appoggiaturas.

The student is advised to analyze the first Prelude from the "Well-Tempered Clavichord"; the manner of showing its harmonic basis being given in the measures quoted below. In the fine example from Wagner, observe which 7ths are prepared and which are not; also that in the third measure from the end the IV⁷ chord in C major is chromatically changed.

BACH: "Well-Tempered Clavichord," 1st Prelude

WAGNER: 1st act of "Die Meistersinger"

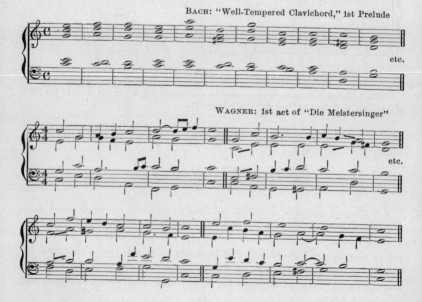

143. To turn now to the old strict rule as regards preparation: it will be conceded that all of the following 7th chords are harsh, when sounded alone, but that this effect is mitigated by the preparation, through which either the 7th or the root is prolonged from a tone in the preceding chord (*i.e.* one of the two dissonant tones is prepared). At the same time there are differences as to the degree of harshness: I⁷ and IV⁷ being more marked in that way than the others, because of the interval of a major 7th; while II⁷, III⁷, and VI⁷ are smoother, with their interval of a minor 7th. It must not be understood from this that I⁷ and IV⁷ are less useful, for that very quality of extreme dissonance makes them perhaps even more interesting factors, as their resolution is doubly agreeable when it does come.

Secondary chords of the 7th in Major Scales.

NOTE. Observe that the chord of the 7th on the IVth degree of the major scale is not resolved above in the same manner as the others, the reason being that by the root ascending a 4th (or descending a 5th) we shall double the leading-tone, a thing only tolerable in a sequence.

It is more symmetrical to have the root and 7th resolve as above, in all of the chords, the 7th moving downward and the root upward.

The rule illustrated in the foregoing may be summed up as follows:

Either THE 7TH IS PROLONGED IN THE SAME VOICE FROM THE PRECEDING CHORD;

Or THE ROOT IS SO PROLONGED, IN WHICH LATTER CASE THE 7TH USUALLY ENTERS DESCENDING BY STEP.

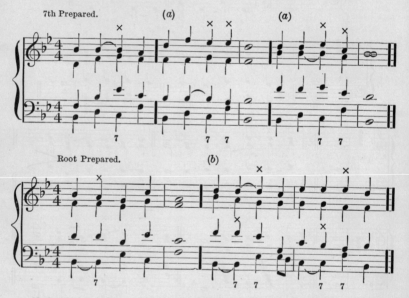

Notice that in (a) and (b) the 7th chord is followed by another dissonance (chord of the 7th); we see that the 7th chord is not necessarily resolved into a consonance, thereby acquiring a resting-point, but that we may have two or more chords of the 7th in succession (§ 147).

When these chords are prepared, as indicated above, this strict treatment of them results in something more rigid than anything with which we have so far become acquainted, when their regular resolution follows.

144. In the normal resolution

(1) THE 7TH NATURALLY DESCENDS ONE DEGREE;

(2) THE ROOT ASCENDS A 4TH (OR DESCENDS A 5TH);

(3) THE THIRD USUALLY DESCENDS A 3D (BUT IS PROLONGED INTO THE NEXT CHORD, IF THAT BE A SECONDARY CHORD OF THE 7TH ALSO);

(4) THE 5TH USUALLY DESCENDS ONE DEGREE;

(5) THE ROOT MAY BE DOUBLED, BUT THE 7TH MUST NEVER BE.[1]

On examining the above examples, it will be found that the 3d cannot progress by ascending without producing a bad leading of the voices, but we have in the following an illustration of an upward progression of the 5th, in which the effect is musical, and the leading of the tenor unusually good.

145. In minor scales we are restricted in applying the usual resolution, by the augmented intervals;

so that I⁷ and IV⁷ are impracticable resolved in this way, but II°⁷, III^×⁷, and VI⁷ are good and extremely useful, *e.g.*

GOLDMARK: "Sakuntala" Overture

---

[1] The 7th, being a sensitive tone, is unfit for doubling.

BRAHMS: Song, "Minnelied"

NOTE. The chord of the 7th on the second degree often enters in such a way that a preferable leading of the voices is obtained by omitting its 5th.

Are better than

In a major key these 5ths would be consecutive perfect ones.

146. The irregular resolutions are that —

(a) The 7th may be prolonged into the next chord, the course taken by the other voices also being changed,

in which case the resolution is either delayed, or abandoned altogether:

(b) it may sometimes ascend,

and in this case the tone to which it naturally would have resolved is taken by another voice. (p. 94, §113.)

(c) The root may be prolonged into the next chord;

(d) The root may ascend by an interval other than the 4th.

A secondary 7th chord may be preceded by a dominant 7th chord or one of its inversions, by a diminished 7th chord or one of its inversions, or by another secondary 7th chord (§ 147) or one of its inversions; it may also be followed by any one of those chords. Most of these points have been illustrated in preceding examples, but for completeness the following are also given:

SUCCESSIVE CHORDS OF THE SECONDARY 7TH

147. These chords of the 7th are frequently used in succession, the result being good and strong when not too many appear at one time (for it is easy to let this device take the place of something better, that would demand more thought on the composer's part). Excepting the sequence, there is no chord progression that is so fixed in its treatment as this; for it is obvious, from the structure of the succeeding chords, that *there will in each one be a 7th to be prepared at the same moment that the 7th in another voice, which has just been prepared in the preceding chord, is being resolved. From the leading of the voices it will also be the case that the root will be doubled in every alternate chord.*

Notice in the preceding page that the chords of the 7th are alternately complete and incomplete; that the sequence could be continued indefinitely, and comes to an end simply to make a rounded musical phrase; it is seldom that so many successive chords of this kind are found.   At × observe the exchange of the 7th of the chord from alto to bass, and the resulting final resolution in the bass (*cf.* Inversions of secondary 7th chords).   (§ 150)

Whenever these chords seem too harsh, it may be that a different arrangement of the voices will mitigate that effect.   Do not be satisfied with trying one way, but write the succession so that the complete chord is the first and third of the group and so on, and also so that it is the second and fourth, etc., and then compare.

The above example is more dissonant written as follows (*a*), and in (*b*) we also see that the question of open or close position must be considered.

WAGNER: "Die Meistersinger" Overture
(VON BÜLOW's arrangement)

In the above splendid example, the harmonic basis of the 7th chords is of course this

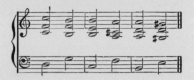

A great gain in freedom will be found now that we have added the
secondary 7ths to our stock of chords, and in Chapter XXXII we shall see
that still more plasticity is obtained by employing their inversions also.

NOTE.   Passing tones (§ 103) may occur on the accented parts of the measure also, and
are in this case called *accented passing tones*.   The following illustration will show the difference in effect (0 indicating the passing tones).

Accented and unaccented passing-tones are indicated in the exercises by short slurs;
the student is recommended to introduce these tones in moderation, when that can be done
with naturalness.

CHAPTER XXXI

EXERCISES INTRODUCING SECONDARY 7TH CHORDS

148. WRITE at least some of the exercises on four staves.   Write each exercise twice;
first preparing all the secondary 7ths, and the second time finding out whether any of them may
well enter without preparation, then comparing the two versions.   When there are successive
chords of the 7th, find the arrangement of voices by which the alternate chords will sound
best.

Soprano melodies to be harmonized.   (Secondary chords of the 7th are indicated by the ×.)

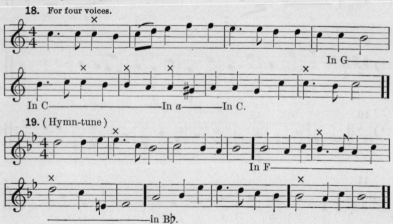

BASS MELODIES TO BE HARMONIZED

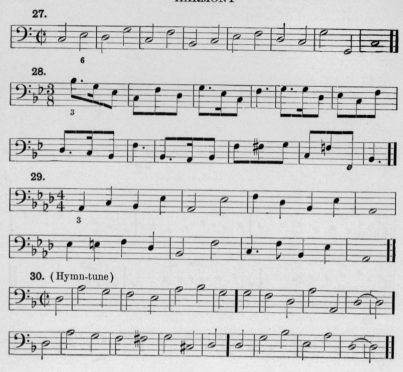

CHAPTER XXXII

INVERSIONS OF THE SECONDARY SEVENTH CHORDS

149. For the use of these inversions without preparation, *cf.* § **141**. If they are introduced in accordance with the <u>stricter rules</u>, we shall have the same preparation of either 7th or root as when the chord is in its un-inverted form. The 7th will have the same regular resolution as before, but the root will be prolonged into the next chord, being in an inner voice.

Free entrance, without preparation

150. From the above it will be seen that either (b) the 7th or (a) the root may be prepared; that the 7th regularly descends one diatonic tone. In (c) is an irregular resolution, by which the 7th is prolonged into the next chord, the root ascending one diatonic tone; in (d) we see how these inversions are used in sequences. With all chords of the 7th, dominant, leading-tone, and secondary, a 7th chord is often followed by an inversion of itself, and an inversion is often followed by the uninverted chord of the 7th or by another inversion of the same chord; the 7th is then transferred from one voice to another, being usually finally resolved in the last chord or inversion. The chord of the 7th, or any inversion, may be repeated, the 7th being exchanged in a similar manner from one voice to another.

The 7th occasionally ascends to the 3d in the following tonic chord, its resolution (prolongation) being taken by another voice.

NOTE. Attention must be called to a progression of frequent occurrence with both dominant and secondary 7th chords, which demands great care. The fault that easily can be made is shown in the following; musical and right ways of handling the chords being also indicated.

151. In the following illustrations we see what powerful and interesting factors **the** chords of the 7th are, and how effectively they may be used in succession.

BEETHOVEN: Sonata, op. 2, No. 1

GRIEG: Gavotte from the Suite "Aus Holberg's Zeit"

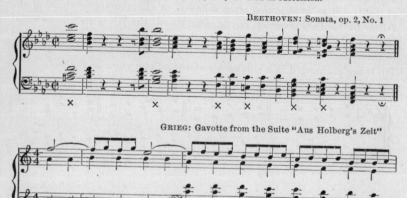

SCHUMANN: Song, "Ich grolle nicht"

CHOPIN: Prelude (Op. 28, No. 4)

HANDEL: "Joshua"

152. Observe the following directions faithfully. *With a secondary chord of the 7th, always be sure which tone is the 7th and which the root; with an inversion, count upward from the bass, ascertaining what the notes in the chord* ARE *as the chord stands, and then what are the* 7TH AND ROOT OF THE ORIGINAL UNINVERTED CHORD.

We have, e.g., in [music] *the notes F-A-C-D; the original chord of the 7th was D-F-A-C, D being the root, and C the 7th.*

Write every exercise twice; first preparing all the secondary 7ths and their inversions, and the second time finding out whether any of them may enter to advantage without preparation; after this, comparing the two versions.

CHAPTER XXXIII

EXERCISES INTRODUCING INVERSIONS OF SECONDARY SEVENTHS

153. (Always find the root and 7th of the uninverted chord.)

SOPRANO MELODIES TO BE HARMONIZED

(In each of these are secondary chords of the 7th and their inversions; some of them, though not all, are marked by the ×.)

In D————————————In A————————In d—

In A————————In D.

BASS MELODIES TO BE HARMONIZED

(Introduce inversions of secondary 7ths in each exercise.)

21.

In G.————

22.

23.

24.

25.

26.

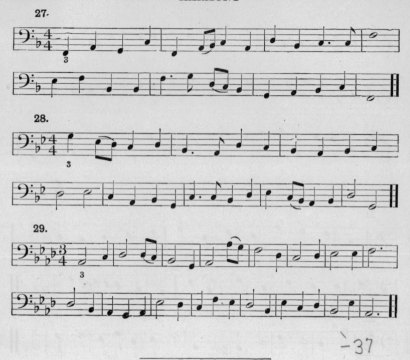

CHAPTER XXXIV

CHORDS OF THE NINTH

154. WE have now discussed the chords most used, and the student is advised to review the preceding chapters. It will be well to write on four staves, and to transpose some of the exercises, introducing passing tones (both accented and unaccented) and auxiliary tones in moderation. It is also recommended that a beginning be made in the use of the C clefs (alto and tenor).[1] THE STUDENT IS NOW READY FOR INVESTIGATION ON HIS OWN ACCOUNT, IN LOOKING UP INSTANCES OF THE EMPLOYMENT OF VARIOUS CHORDS AND CHORD SUCCESSIONS; the works of the masters from Bach to Schumann exist in editions so inexpensive that it is easy to form gradually an adequate collection of them, and not only to become acquainted with the best literature, but to gain a living sense of harmonic questions as they present themselves in the music of the great composers.

[1] The C clef has been used for all the voices except the bass, and is still much employed in orchestral music (for the viola, violoncello, bassoon, trombones, etc.). On whichever line of the staff it is employed, it designates the tone ; alto and tenor are consequently the same as and .

will appear as follows, when written with these clefs.

155. Before entering upon the subject of this chapter, we must understand the fundamental idea of *the suspension* and *the appoggiatura*.

When any tone of a chord is delayed in moving to that tone of the following chord to which it would naturally proceed, by being prolonged into the following chord (of which it does not form a harmonic part), a dissonance is produced requiring a resolution. *The tone referred to of the first chord is then said to be* SUSPENDED, and is regularly resolved by later proceeding upward or downward to its proper tone in the second chord.

156. An APPOGGIATURA is a tone not suspended, foreign to the chord with which it occurs; in other words it is a tone dissonant from the chord, and must move diatonically downward or upward in its resolution.

Passing and auxiliary tones have been defined (§ § **103, 104, 147**).

THE CHORD OF THE NINTH

157. This chord is formed by adding another 3d to a chord of the 7th, just as we formed the chord of the 7th by adding another 3d to the triad. It clearly is possible to construct seven such chords in every major and minor key, but many of them have no harmonic consequence; most of those which are available enter by means of suspensions, appoggiaturas, and passing or auxiliary tones.

158. The dominant chord of the 9th is the one chiefly employed, and properly used is productive of admirable results. Our attention will therefore be chiefly directed to it, before we consider chords of the 9th on other degrees of the scale. It occurs in major keys[1] (in which the 9th is usually major, though occasionally chromatically altered to a minor one, Ex. 2), and in minor keys (in which the 9th is usually minor, sometimes being chromatically altered to a major one, Ex. 4).

159. As there are five tones in this chord, one must be omitted in four-part writing, while no doubling is allowable. The root and 9th must always be present; if the 7th is omitted, the 9th appears rather as an appogiatura or suspension (*e.g.* p. 165, Ex. 12, 13), the chord being hardly to be properly classed as a real chord of the 9th; the 7th being present, either the 3d or the 5th must be omitted, the result being more characteristic if we have the 3d in the chord. When the 3d is omitted, however, that note sometimes appears in the following chord (3 and 4 *seq.*)

[1] A chord of the dominant 9th, standing by itself, is even stronger in giving a feeling of tonality than is the dominant 7th; it not only fixes the key but the mode (with the rare exceptions caused by chromatic changes, as mentioned above). It is an interesting fact that this chord is really a combination of the dominant and leading tone 7th chords.

160. *The 9th may be prolonged from a preceding chord, or may enter by step or by skip, not needing to be prepared; its customary resolution is one degree down, the root ascending to the tonic, the 7th descending one degree, the 3d (if present) ascending to the tonic, and the 5th (if present) either ascending or descending.*

In another common resolution, the 9th descends while the other voices remain stationary, the second chord thus being a chord of the dominant 7th.[1]

The 9th sometimes proceeds to another tone (not the root) of the following chord of the 7th, and may also be followed by another triad than the tonic (Ex. 12).

161. The 9th not infrequently resolves upward.

---

[1] Strictly speaking, the chord of the 9th does not resolve in this and similar cases (Ex. 4 and 8 (a) and (b)); the interval of the 9th does resolve, but the chord-resolution takes place finally through the dominant 7th chord.

Instead of resolving upward to the 3d of the chord, it may descend to that tone an octave lower, making a skip of a 7th;

or may leap to another tone of the same harmony.

In the following it is used as a passing tone, in an ascending and a descending passage.

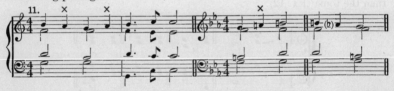

Finally, the 9th may be irregularly prolonged into the next (different) chord; see Ex. 7.

Observe in Ex. 2 the minor 9th in a major key, entering by preparation; in Ex. 4 the major 9th in a minor key, entering by skip; in Ex. 3, 8 (a) the omitted 3d, which is given us in the chord of resolution; in Ex. 5 (a) (b) the different resolutions of the 5th in order to avoid consecutive 5ths; that in Ex. 4, 8 (a) it may be properly considered an appoggiatura, and in 11 as a passing tone; that in Exs. 2, 3, 6, 8 (b) it is suspended; that in 7, 9, 10 it moves in some cases by a skip. (Cf. § 165.)

NOTE. Something should be said here concerning a view held by many theorists, especially in England and France. It is briefly this, that chords of the leading-tone **7th** in major and minor are to be regarded as chords of the 9th with the root (or "generator") omitted, and that the first inversion of the leading-tone triad is a dominant 7th chord with its root omitted.

This opens an interesting field for speculation, and is to a certain extent justified by facts in acoustics, but hardly important to the student who is learning about chords and their uses. From a musical point of view, the value of this theory seems questionable when one considers that the tone F of the following chord of the 6th will nearly always ascend, and may even be doubled (in which latter case one F will ascend), neither of which things is true of the 7th in the 7th chord of which this chord of the 6th is supposed to be a part.

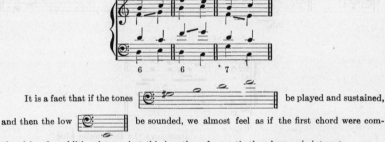

It is a fact that if the tones [music] be played and sustained,

and then the low [music] be sounded, we almost feel as if the first chord were completed by the additional tone; but this is rather of acoustic than harmonic interest.

162. It is most often the case that the 9th is placed in the soprano; it may, however, be in either alto or tenor. The only thing absolutely necessary is that in pure four-part writing *the 9th shall always appear above the root and be distant at least a 9th from it*, for the result otherwise will be excessively harsh.

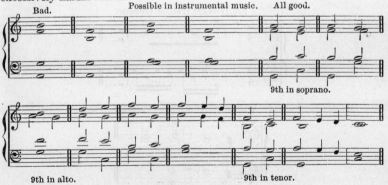

The above are all good in minor keys also.

A fine example of the 9th in the alto, with the 3d above it, is seen in the extract from the "Meistersinger" overture (§ 147).

etc.

9th.

163. Some examples of this chord follow, illustrating various points of entrance and of resolution.

WAGNER: "Lohengrin"

9th.

SCHUBERT: Sonata, Op. 42

DEBUSSY: "La Demoiselle Élue"

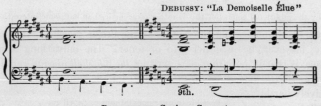

9th.

BEETHOVEN: C minor Concerto

9th.

BEETHOVEN: Sonata, Op. 53

9th.

CHADWICK: "Lovely Rosabelle"

CHOPIN: B♭ minor Sonata

MENDELSSOHN: Chorale

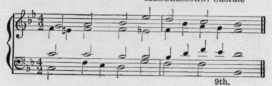

SCHUMANN: Toccata

In these last three examples the 9th appears in an authentic cadence. We now have an illustration of successive chords of the 9th, as well as one of successive chords of the 7th. It is but fair to say that they are to be regarded as specimens of an exceedingly free treatment of these chords; the question of pure part-writing does not enter. The extract from Debussy is from an opera, and in music for the stage far greater liberty is allowable than with what is called absolute music: the same is true about the piano piece of Grieg.

DEBUSSY: "Pelléas et Mélisande"

GRIEG: Nocturne, Op. 54, No. 4

INVERSIONS OF THE CHORD OF THE DOMINANT NINTH

164. There are four inversions,

of which (*a*) and (*c*) are very useful, (*b*) being available when resulting naturally from the voice-leading, but the last inversion not worth consideration, on account of its harshness (§ **162**).

CHORDS OF THE NINTH ON OTHER DEGREES

165. We have seen that the chord of the dominant 9th may enter by preparation, by step, or by skip; that it may be resolved by prolongation into the next chord, by descending, or by ascending. This is largely the case with 9th chords on other degrees of the scale. These nearly always appear as suspensions, appoggiaturas, passing-tones or auxiliary tones, but their treatment is more restricted; the chord of the dominant 9th resembles that of the dominant 7th in its resolution, but such is not necessarily the case with other chords of the 9th. *It should also be said that, as the interval of the 9th really forms an integral part of the chord, the requirements of the definition of the term suspension are not met (§ 207); it is more logical to say that the 9th is prepared, as 7ths are prepared (p. 132), and to consider that we do not have a true suspension.*

The following examples are given to show how these chords of the 9th appear (*a*) through suspension, (*b*) as appoggiaturas, (*c*) as passing-tones, (*d*) as auxiliary tones.

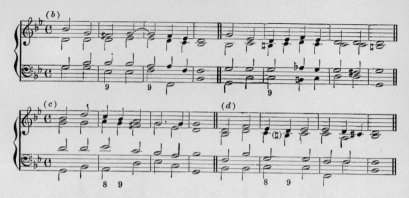

In (*a*) the 9th may also resolve upward, or move downward by skip; in (*c*) it may be prolonged into the next chord.

The chord of the 9th on the super-tonic is often used in a cadence as follows, and occasionally with the chromatic change indicated in (*f*), in which latter case it becomes a dominant 9th derived from the dominant key.

BACH: Chromatic Fantasie

BACH: Preludio con fuga. (Peters Ed. No. 207)

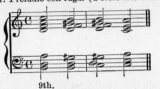

9th.

BACH: Well-Tempered Clavichord, Vol. I, 22d Fugue

etc.

9th.

HENSCHEL : "Requiem"

9th.

166. The secondary chords of the 9th are flexible in treatment, although great care must be taken that the leading of the voices is pure and musical; the inherent harshness of many of these chords is softened by the manner in which they are introduced, as indicated above. *It should be observed that the occurrence of the interval of a 9th does not of itself indicate a real chord of the 9th.* In the following the note G is a simple appoggiatura in one voice, and the chord is really a chord of the 6th.

CHAPTER XXXV

EXERCISES WITH CHORDS OF THE NINTH

167.

1.

2.

3.

4.

5.

6.

7.

8.

9. *Adagio*

Chords of the 9th are indicated by a ×; in some exercises (e. g. No. 12) the 7th is to be omitted.

CHAPTER XXXVI

CHORDS OF THE ELEVENTH AND THIRTEENTH

168. No one can say what will be the future of music on the harmonic side; judging from the past there will be further development, at least in the direction of greater freedom in the use of chords. In the history of music we find at different periods the ecclesiastical modes giving way to our present scale system, the mediæval vagueness of tonality abandoned for our modern definite feeling, and a purely contrapuntal way of working developed, by the growth of harmonic understanding, into the methods employed in the master works of Bach. We know approximately when the use of suspensions became common, when the dominant 7th was allowed to appear without preparation, when the authentic cadence came into ordinary use. During the last century freedom has been gained in the use of secondary 7ths without preparation, in the introduction of chromatic passing-tones, etc., and of chromatically changed chords, and in the manner of regarding the tritone and the cross relation; the chord of the 9th has been granted its place, as an independent factor, in the family of chords. Investigation and experiment are still going on.

169. With the chords of the 11th and 13th, however, we seem to have come to the end of independent chords. From our present point of view they appear to exist mainly through suspension, or by means of appoggiaturas, and passing and auxiliary tones. But, although a discussion of them might be left until later, in the chapters on suspension, etc., it seems preferable to make a brief statement here as regards their use.

CHORD OF THE ELEVENTH

170. In the same way that we get the chord of the 9th by the addition of a 3d to the chord of the 7th, so we obtain the chord of the 11th by adding another 3d to the chord of the 9th. A chord of the 11th can theoretically be erected on any tone of a major or minor scale; but, as is the case with the chord of the 9th, the chord of the 11th with the dominant for its root is the one most employed.

Observe that in the examples given, the chord enters in the manner described in § **169.**

171. It is clear that two of these six tones must be omitted in four-part writing; that the 11th is merely the 4th placed an octave higher; and that it will consequently often appear as a suspension (the 4th being regarded in suspensions as a dissonant tone that must be resolved); examples of this (a), as well as of the 11th entering as an appoggiatura (b), and passing (c) and auxiliary tone (d) follow. The 11th is resolved either downward or upward.

In the following example of this chord, with an unusual resolution, we see how easy it is for theorists to differ; for it is also quite naturally explained as being a chord of the dominant 7th, placed below an inverted pedal (the tone D of the soprano; *cf.* the chapter on the Pedal).

SCHUMANN: Novellette, Op. 21, No. 8

172. It may also occur together with a suspension of another voice; as the 11th is the same tone as the 4th (an octave higher), the 3d is of course omitted in the dissonant chord, and we must choose whether the 5th, 7th, or 9th is to be also omitted.

MENDELSSOHN: "Midsummer Night's Dream" Overture

11th.

CHORD OF THE THIRTEENTH

173. By adding yet another 3d to the chord of the **11th**, we obtain the chord of the 13th.

7th.   9th.   11th.   13th.

The addition of another 3d to the chord of the 13th brings us to the tone two octaves above the root, and therefore to the end of all possible chords, as we should then begin our series of 3ds over again.

174. This chord also usually appears with the dominant for its root, and is logically explained as resulting from a suspension, an appoggiatura, a passing tone or an auxiliary tone.

In four-part writing three of the seven tones of this chord must be omitted. A few examples are given of its most common use.

BEETHOVEN: 9th Symphony

13th (inverted.)

WAGNER: "Der fliegende Holländer"

13th.

WAGNER: Quintet from
" Die Meistersinger "

BRAHMS: Intermezzo, op. 119.

13th.   13th (complete)

WAGNER: "Die Meistersinger" (p. 389)]

GRIEG: Song, "Ein Schwan"

13th.

DEBUSSY: "Pelléas et Mélisande"

9th.   13th.   9th.

In the last example we have this chord used independently; a rare instance. It is given rather to show that experiments are being made in this direction; the result may tend to further emancipation of the chord of the 13th.

SCHUMANN: "Des Abends," Op. 12, No. 1.

9th. 13th. 7th.

(As this is for pianoforte, and the pedal sustains the other tones of the dominant harmony, the chord may be regarded as a true 13th.)

CHAPTER XXXVII

CHROMATICALLY ALTERED CHORDS

175. So far we have been dealing with chords of a definite tonality, which were classified mainly as triads and seventh chords (in either fundamental or inverted position) on the various degrees of the major or the minor scale. We must now enlarge our harmonic vocabulary by studying an important group of chords which are formed by chromatic alteration. The principle is this, that, whenever any voice progresses by a whole tone, the latter may be subdivided into semitones by the introduction of appropriate accidentals, *e.g.*

176. Theoretically, any factor of a triad, or of a 7th or of a 9th chord may be chromatically raised or lowered. Some of these formations will not differ from chords found in a regular scale-series; some are used but rarely, and as passing chords; while others are so frequent in inverted positions that they are felt to have a definite identity and have received appropriate names.

177. The 3d of triads is the factor which decides whether the mode be major or minor; either the root or the 5th may be chromatically altered, but those chords which arise from an alteration of the 5th are decidedly of the most importance, *e.g.*

In (1) we have a major triad with an augmented 5th. As this is an alteration of C–E–G, it may be used as a passing chord in C major, F major, G major. or *e* minor; *i. e.* in keys in which C–E–G is tonic, dominant, subdominant, or submediant triad, *e.g.*

C Major

This triad C–E–G♯ is also found in *a* minor, in that case being not an altered chord, but the regular augmented triad on the third degree; and in that relationship its use, as we have seen (§ 61), is comparatively rare.   Henceforth it will often occur as an altered chord.

Of (2), a minor triad with an augmented 5th, an example will soon be given (p. 175). Although (3) is classified as a diminished triad, it also occurs very frequently as a major triad with an augmented root, used as a passing tone; *e.g.*

(4) A triad with a diminished 5th and a diminished 3d is comparatively rare in its fundamental position (except as a passing chord), but in its first inversion is one of the most useful chromatic harmonies,— the chord of the *augmented sixth; e.g.*

Aug. 6.

(5) A triad with a diminished 5th and a major 3d is sometimes found in the first inversion as a passing chord with striking effect; *e.g.*

CHERUBINI: Requiem for Men's Voices

(6) A minor triad with a lowered 5th is very common; *e.g.*

(7) is sometimes found as a passing chord; *e.g.*

178. Triads with an augmented 5th are also practicable when inverted, *i.e.*, as 6 and 6–4 chords; *e.g.*

179. In like manner with 7th and 9th chords — although theoretically any factor may be altered, the 5th is most frequently so changed; *e.g.*

In this table we have some of the most usual chromatically altered 7th and 9th chords. Certain of these combinations are more common in inversions, and they are generally used in open position; for if the altered 5th and the 7th are near together the effect is usually harsh. (*a*) is a dominant 7th chord with augmented 5th; as a 4–3 chord with the augmented tone in the **bass** it is rare, but all the other positions are common and extremely effective. Observe that by the use of open position the 7th and the altered 5th are kept apart; *e.g.*

(*b*) is extremely rare in fundamental position, but, as a 6–5 chord, is by no means uncommon, and as a 4–3 chord is of great importance; *e.g.*

BACH: St. Matthew Passion

(*c*) a diminished 7th chord with lowered 3d, is often found in fundamental position, and by reason of the diminished 3d, caused by the chromatic alteration, is one of the most expressive chords in music; *e.g.*

BACH: Mass in B minor

MENDELSSOHN: "Hear My Prayer"

VERDI: Requiem

This chord (c) in its first inversion, where the diminished 3d becomes an augmented 6th, is most important, and will be fully treated later; e.g.

Aug. 6
5

(d) is often used as a passing chord; e.g.

(e) and (f), dominant major and minor 9th chords with augmented 5ths, are very common; a beautiful example is given from Wagner.

"Das Rheingold"

The second theme in the first movement of Beethoven's Heroic Symphony affords a remarkable illustration of several chromatically altered chords.

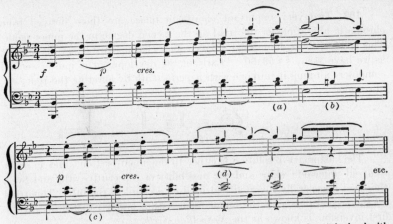

At (*a*) we have a major triad with augmented 5th; at (*b*) a secondary 7th chord with augmented 5th; at (*c*) a minor triad with augmented 5th, and at (*d*) an inverted dominant 7th with augmented root.

180. Although in many cases (as in the examples given above) these altered tones proceed by a semitone, this is not invariably necessary. They may enter by a leap, especially in instrumental music; *e.g.*

SCHUMANN: Song, "Süsser Freund." (Op. 42)

181. As to the progression of these altered tones — when augmented they generally continue to ascend, and when diminished to descend. This is illustrated in all the examples above.

Chromatic alterations are often written enharmonically, partly to secure simplicity in writing and also to conform to the conventional notation of the chromatic scale, in which the seventh degree remains lowered and the fourth degree raised, in both ascending and descending passages; *e.g.*

182. Two very important chords in music are those derived from chromatic alterations of the triad on the second degree in the minor mode. This triad, with its diminished 5th, is a somewhat unsatisfactory dissonance, as we have seen (§ § **58, 60**). Early in the development of music, we find composers altering it into one with a perfect 5th by lowering the root; *e.g.* in *c* minor.

The customary resolution is either to dominant or tonic, and in order to avoid unmelodic skips and the possibility of consecutive 5ths and 8ves, the triad is generally inverted and used as a chord of the 6th. This triad on the second degree of the minor mode with a lowered root, when in the first inversion, is known as the *Neapolitan Sixth*.

183. This altered triad is by no means limited to the first inversion; in instrumental music, especially, it is often found in the fundamental position, or even as a 6–4 chord, *e.g.*

CHOPIN: Prelude No. 20

HÄNDEL: "Messiah"

Von Weber: Overture to "Der Freischütz"

Von Weber: Overture to "Der Freischütz"

184. This triad on the second degree in the minor mode is often altered, by allowing the root to remain as in the key and raising both the 3d and the 5th a semitone, *e.g.*

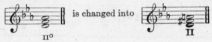

is changed into

We often find phrases like the following.

In the next passage, from Beethoven, we find both of these chromatically altered chords from the second degree used in succession.

Sonata, Op. 31, No. 2

etc.

185. The Neapolitan Sixth, although derived from the minor mode, is often found in the tonic major; here is one characteristic example.

Brahms: "Deutsches Requiem"

etc.

186. The above list of chromatically altered chords is not complete; but for the present it is sufficient for the student to know the more important facts as stated above. Little by little it is possible, through harmonic analysis and the study of modern compositions, to become familiar with varied effects, which can be explained only by a broad application of these principles.

In modern **music** passages like the following are of frequent occurrence, the free alterations in the chords being evident. The bass is a tonic pedal-point (*cf.* chapter on the Pedal.)

187. The following melody is to be harmonized with the aid of altered chords.

Let the student first play and sing this melody, then harmonize it, and finally compare with the following version.

      (a)   (b)   (c)   (d)

At (*a*) we have a secondary 7th chord with a raised 5th; at (*b*) a third inversion of a secondary 7th with a lowered 5th; at (*c*) a dominant 7th with a raised 5th, and at (*d*) a simple triad treated in like manner.

The following interesting passage from a modern symphony shows the dominant 7th chord with the 5th raised and lowered in the same chord in different voices.

TSCHAIKOWSKI: 6th Symphony, (2d movement)

                                         etc.

"The essential fundamental chords are but few, and must remain so, but the combinations which can be made to represent them on the polyphonic principle are almost infinite. By the use of chromatic passing and preliminary notes, by retardations, and by simple chromatic alterations of the notes of chords according to their melodic significance, combinations are arrived at such as puzzled and do puzzle theorists who regard harmony as so many unchangeable lumps of chords which cannot be admitted in music unless a fundamental bass can be found for them.   Thus the chord of the augmented 6th is probably nothing more than the modification of a melodic progression of one or two parts at the point where naturally they would be either a major or minor 6th from one another, the downward tendency of the one and the upward tendency of the other causing them to be respectively flattened and sharpened to make them approach nearer to the notes to which they are moving. . . . The actual number of essential chords has remained the same as it was when Monteverde indicated the nature of the dominant 7th by using it without preparation, unless a single exception be made in favor of the chord of the major 9th and its sister the minor 9th, both of which Helmholtz acknowledges may be taken as representatives of the lower note or root."   (From the article on 'Harmony' by Parry, in Grove's 'Dictionary of Music.')

CHAPTER XXXVIII

EXERCISES IN ALTERED CHORDS

188. 5, 5♯ indicate that the 5th is first a diatonic note, and in the next chord is raised chromatically (§ 51.)

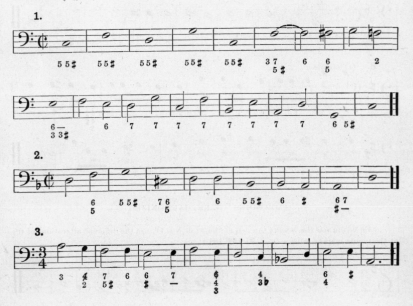

MELODIES TO BE HARMONIZED

(In No. 10 use the Neapolitan 6th at the ✕; in No. 11, use the different alterations of II° at the points marked with a ✕: *cf.* §§ **182–184**.)

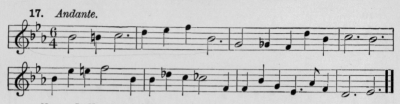

17. *Andante.*

NOTE. In Nos. 9–17 it is sometimes the case that there are to be chromatic changes in another voice besides the soprano.

Bass melodies to be harmonized; altered chords are indicated by the ×, and passing or auxiliary tones by the slur; the chromatically altered tone may appear at any place in the measure.

18.

19.

20.

21.

CHAPTER XXXIX

AUGMENTED CHORDS

189. WE find in music three very important chords, the augmented 6th, the augmented 6–4–3, and the augmented 6–5–3. *In each of these chords the characteristic interval is the augmented 6th, which is always caused* *by chromatic alteration,* for the major and minor scales contain only major and minor 6ths.   The interval of an augmented 6th may be formed from a major 6th either by lowering the lower tone or by raising the upper one, *e.g.*

Major 6th. Aug. 6th. Major 6th. Aug. 6th.

and from a minor 6th by altering both the upper and the lower tone at the same time, *e.g.*

Minor 6th. Aug. 6th.

190. *In resolving these chords the general tendency is for the voices which contain the augmented 6th to continue expanding into a perfect octave,* example (*a*); occasionally each of the voices descends a semitone, as at (*b*); one voice often remains stationary while the other moves, (*c*) and (*d*); sometimes one voice leaps (*e*) and (*f*); it is even possible, although not common, for both voices to converge (*g*).

(*a*)   (*b*)   (*c*)   (*d*)   (*e*)   (*f*)   (*g*)

These resolutions apply to all of the three augmented 6th chords.   Each chord, however, has special points of treatment.

191. 1st. — THE AUGMENTED 6TH CHORD.

As this chord, like any 6th chord, consists of but three different tones, in four-part writing the question of doubling has to be settled.   *As both of the tones forming the augmented 6th have strong tendencies along certain lines, and moreover are very characteristic in sound, they are practically never doubled. It is the invariable practice to double the 3d, counting from the bass of the augmented 6th chord.*   The usual groupings are as follows:

In free pianoforte writing and in all instrumental music with more than four parts, these considerations as to doubling do not remain in force, *e.g.*

BEETHOVEN: "Prometheus"

192. In introducing and resolving this chord, the student is strongly advised not to raise the question of tonality. Tonality can rarely be settled by a single chord (much less a chromatically altered one) but nearly always depends on the context (p. 154). *In the majority of cases, augmented chords resolve to chords which we recognize as either tonic or dominant,* and thus may be said to be more nearly related to some keys than to others. They are so freely used, however, especially in modern music, that it is not always practicable to settle just what is their origin. This augmented 6th chord. for instance, may be used in all the following keys.

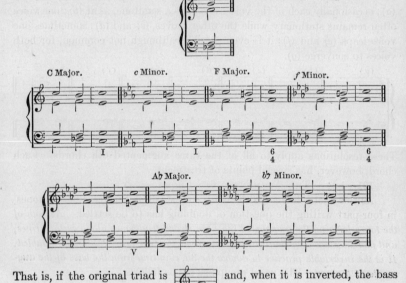

That is, if the original triad is [music] and, when it is inverted, the bass

is lowered, [music] the augmented 6th chord resulting would be re-

lated to C major or *c* minor. On the other hand, if the original triad were

which can be found on the fourth degree of *f* minor or the sec-

ond degree of A♭ major, and the 6th of the inverted triad were raised,

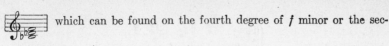 the augmented 6th chord would be related to *f* minor, (F

major) or A♭ major.

193. We cite a few examples.

BEETHOVEN: 2d Symphony (Larghetto)

SPOHR: "Fall of Babylon"   MOZART: Symphony in G Minor

SCHUMANN: Humoreske, Op. 20

194. These augmented 6th chords are also occasionally used **in the 2d**
inversion, generally as passing 6–4 chords; *e.g.*

Observe the augmented 4th in 6♭ ; the figuring for these augmented chords is 6+, 6+, 4+
  4+   5   3
to distinguish them from the inversions of triads and 7th chords, in which the 6th is not
augmented.

195. The chord of the augmented 6th, 4th, and 3d.

A 6–4–3 chord is always the second inversion of a dominant 7th or of some secondary 7th chord. Whenever the major or minor 6th of certain 6–4–3 chords is changed into an augmented 6th by the introduction of accidentals we have an augmented 6–4–3 chord, *e.g.*

196. Observe that, however the augmented 6–4–3 may be formed, the intervals from the bass are always *a major 3d, an augmented 4th, and an augmented 6th; in fact the true name should be chord of the augmented 6th, augmented 4th, and 3d.*

Augmented 6–4–3 chords may be erected on any given tone, and as to their tonality (from the standpoint of their derivation), they are related to the dominant 7th chord in both major and minor, or to the secondary 7th chords on the 2d, 3d, 6th, and 7th degrees in major, and the 2d in minor. This is made clear by examples (*a*), (*b*) and (*c*) above. Like the augmented 6th chord they generally resolve either to tonic or dominant harmony, although freer resolutions are by no means uncommon.

The following example illustrates some of the most frequent uses of this chord.

From CHADWICK'S Harmony

197. The chromatically altered 7th chords from which the augmented 6-4-3 chords are derived are also found in the fundamental position, as well as in the first and third inversions (*i.e.* as 6-5 and 4-2 chords). These positions are very common in modern music and their effect is always striking. On account of their importance, examples are given of each.

GOUNOD: "Faust"   WAGNER: "Die Meistersinger"

In both these examples we find 7th chords with a lowered 5th in the fundamental position; these chords, if placed in the 2d inversion, would result in augmented 6-4-3 chords. *e.g.*

In the first measure of example (*b*) we also have an augmented 6-4-3 chord on D♭.

VERDI: "Requiem"

In this last example we find the first inversion of a dominant 7th chord with lowered fifth (p. 173), *e.g.*

In the last chord of the second measure is an illustration of a very important point, not only in augmented chords but in all chromatic alterations. The chord is really an augmented 6-4-3, and would ordinarily have been written;

in order, however, to preserve the symmetry of the ascending bass the Db is enharmonically changed to C♯.

One more very characteristic example is given of this first inversion.

CÉSAR FRANCK: Prelude.

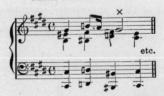

As in the example from Verdi **above, the** original chord is 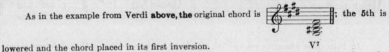 ; the 5th is lowered and the chord placed in its first inversion.

For an illustration of the last inversion of this chord we have the following from the same Prelude of Franck.

In the first measure we see the chord  placed in its third inversion (*i.e.*

as a 4–2 chord); in the second measure the same chord is used in the more common way as

a regular augmented 6–4–3, *i.e.*

The following striking passage contains both an augmented 6–4–3 chord, and also the
first inversion of the original 7th chord.

BRAHMS: Sonata in *f* minor.

THE AUGMENTED 6–5–3 CHORD

198. Whenever the major or minor 6th in the first inversion (6–5) of
certain 7th chords is changed by chromatic alteration into an augmented
6th, we have a chord of the augmented 6th, 5th, and 3d, *e.g.*

199. As to the practical use of this chord, it may be introduced in the
freest possible manner, provided the leading of the voices be good, and it
is by no means necessary that it should be preceded by the unaltered 6–5
chord. Like the augmented 6th chords just discussed, it has many and
varied resolutions, although some of them are more common than others
and have more natural key affinities.

200. In regard to the derivation of this chord (quite apart from its
entrance and progression in any given context), the most useful view is to

consider that it is the first inversion of a diminished 7th chord with a chromatically lowered 3d. Many French and German theorists treat all the augmented chords as inverted forms of chromatically altered dominant harmony. These chords are often found grouped together in passages like the following:

i.e. the chords in (*a*) are derived from this dominant chord and those in (*b*) from which is an altered dominant chord on the

2d degree (or the dominant of the dominant).

201. The usual resolutions of this chord are analogous to those of the two other augmented chords. Exceptional resolutions will be shown in examples.

When an augmented 6–5 chord resolves directly to a triad as at (*a*), the consecutive 5ths so caused are generally avoided in strict four-part writing for voices, although not infrequently found in instrumental music, *e.g.*

BEETHOVEN: Sonata No. 1
for violoncello and piano

In the following we have two resolutions of this chord in succession;

SCHUBERT: Fantasie, Op 78

while in the next we are shown the beautiful effect producible by the different chromatic alterations of the same tones.

GOUNOD: Introduction to "Faust"

In this augmented 6th chord the student must constantly be on the watch for changes in notation, as when the chord resolves to a major 6-4 chord the perfect 5th is almost always written as a doubly augmented 4th, *e.g.*

i.e. D♯ is written instead of E♭ in order to preserve the symmetry of the ascending soprano.

The following passage is a beautiful example of this doubly augmented 4th; the resolution also is somewhat unusual — to the first inversion of the submediant triad.

SCHUMANN: Novellette, Op. 21, No. 7

202. From the outset the student must recognize the fact that *any augmented 6-5 chord is in sound identical with a dominant 7th chord;* e.g. if this chord be played by itself we cannot tell whether an augmented chord is meant or a dominant 7th (p. 94). Great use is made of this enharmonic relationship in modulating between remote keys (*cf.* Chapter XLV), for obviously chord (*a*) can be approached from several of the sharp keys, *e.g.* G and D, and with the implied enharmonic change (*b*), can be directed toward A♭, D♭, *f*, etc. The student should look up for himself examples of this modulation in standard compositions.

203. Like the two preceding chords, the augmented 6–5 chord is very common in the fundamental position (*i.e.* as a 7th chord with a diminished 3d) and also in the two other inversions (4–3 and 2). Examples are cited of each.

WAGNER: Prelude to "Lohengrin"

In this passage we find a chromatically altered 7th chord used in the fundamental position.

This chord placed in the first inversion would give a regular augmented 6–5, *e.g.*

The introductory chords of Schubert's wonderfully dramatic song "Am Meer" furnish a striking example of this chord in the second inversion.

Here we see another case of the enharmonic notation spoken of above, for D♯ is written instead of E♭ on account of the upward resolution. The 7th chord in its original position is

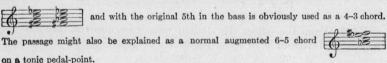

and with the original 5th in the bass is obviously used as a 4–3 chord. The passage might also be explained as a normal augmented 6–5 chord on a tonic pedal-point.

The following passage gives us both the third inversion (chord of the 2d) and another second inversion, the original chord being

CHOPIN: Nocturne, Op. 15, No. 3

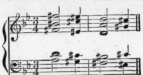

204. Now that the fundamental facts in regard to this chord have been presented, its use will best be learned by a careful analysis of examples from musical literature. A few are cited and others should be sought for. A thorough knowledge of all the augmented chords is indispensable for an insight into the subtle harmonies of modern music.

SCHUBERT: Impromptu, Op. 142, No. 2

SCHUMANN: "Bunte Blätter," Op. 99, No. 14

The above passage is unique in its abundance of augmented harmonies, both in fundamental position and in inversions. Observe that the first two measures are on a double pedal.

GOUNOD: "Faust," Act I — "Faust," Act III

These last examples are interesting, the former on account of the downward resolution of the augmented interval, the latter for the combination of a suspended tone with the third inversion of an altered 7th chord, e.g. Observe the subtle chromatic resolution.

In the passage from Tschaikowski observe the bold downward leap of the B♭.

In analyzing this beautiful phrase of Dvořák, let the student ask himself what is the position of the chord and also explain the notation.

205. In harmonizing melodies (Chapter XL, Ex. 7–24) it is helpful to know that the augmented 6, augmented 6–4–3 and augmented 6–5 chords are frequently to be derived from inversions of the fourth triad, second chord of the 7th and fourth chord of the 7th, respectively, of the minor scale, their ordinary resolutions being the following (but *cf.* §§ **192, 196 198, 201**).

The student is reminded, however, that these chords are derivable in various ways (§§ **192, 196, 198**); THEY ARE THEREFORE VERY USEFUL IN MODULATION.

CHAPTER XL

EXERCISES WITH AUGMENTED CHORDS AND THEIR INVERSIONS

$$\left(\begin{matrix} 6+, & 6+, & 6+ \\ & 4+, & 5 \\ & 3 & \end{matrix}\right)$$

206. AUGMENTED triads being marked by a ✕, the same method is pursued with the augmented chords. A distinction is thus made in figured basses between these chords and such as are indicated by ♭6, ♭5, ♭4/3 (§ 194). In the soprano melodies some, not all, of the augmented chords are marked by a ✕; in a few of the bass melodies they are also indicated in the same way, figures not being given in Ex. 7–10. Augmented skips are permitted in any voice.

EXERCISES FOR THREE VOICES. The $\frac{6+}{4+}$ chord can be used by having a voice sing as
follows (§ 200):

Augmented chords are marked by a ×).

CHAPTER XLI

SUSPENSIONS

207. HERETOFORE in our work all the voices have progressed simultaneously from one chord to the next, although one or more of the tones were often harmonic factors common to each chord and sometimes held over into the second chord from the first one. We must now become familiar with *a rhythmic device, by which the prolongation of tones into a chord to which they do not belong delays the entrance of one or more of the logical factors in that chord; in other words, parts of two different chords are momentarily heard together,* and the dissonance and rhythmic disturbance caused by this harmonic dislocation are felt to be logical, when the delayed voices move on to the tones which would otherwise have originally been sounded.

If, *e.g.* instead of having the voices move as follows,

we delay the entrance of the 3d in the second chord by holding over the **F**,

while the other voices proceed to their positions in the next chord, a genuine suspension is formed, in which the dissonant and rhythmic elements are

plainly felt.[1]   Thus, in the preceding, the tone F is delayed in its progression
to E by being *suspended,* while the rest of the harmony changes.   The
entrance of such a tone as part of the first chord is called the *preparation*
(a); the holding it over into the following chord to which it does not belong is the *suspension itself* (b); and the ultimate progression of the suspended tone to its proper place in the chord is the *resolution* (c).

208.   Suspension, like chromatic alteration, is a principle of very
broad application, and our best approach to the subject is the general
statement that a suspension may be formed by delaying the downward or
upward progression of any factor of a triad, or seventh, or ninth chord;
this effect may take place in any voice and in any position of the chord,
fundamental or inverted.   When the examples are studied it will be seen,
however, that some of these suspensions are much better, and hence more
common, than others.

209.   The laws governing the use of suspensions are few, and extremely
logical and simple; but a thoroughly artistic handling of them is ac-
quired only by considerable practice.   It is obvious that the suspended
tone must invariably be prepared in the same voice in which it is to be
sounded as the dissonance; *e.g.* if we write (a) instead of (b), we have no
suspension at all, but an appoggiatura (Chapter XLIII).

This effect is sometimes called an unprepared suspension, although such a paradoxical
term is questionable.

210.   There is an old rule which, in one form and another, still appears in books upon harmony.   As given in a recent treatise it is as follows:
"If the suspension be tied to its preparation, the latter should be of at
least equal length with the suspension; it may be longer, but must not be
shorter.   When the suspended note is sounded again, this rule is not so
strictly observed."

This academic rule is too sweeping, and is not justified by the practice
of composers; it should therefore be abandoned.   The strongest statement
that can rightly be made is that in a large majority of cases the tone or
preparation is at least as long as that of suspension, and that the rhythmic
effect attained in that way is usually better.   In the following, the tone
of preparation in (a) and (b) is shorter than that of suspension, while in
(c) it is of the same length.

[1] By some theorists those suspensions which resolve upwards are called Retardations;
but this term is an unnecessary fineness in classification.

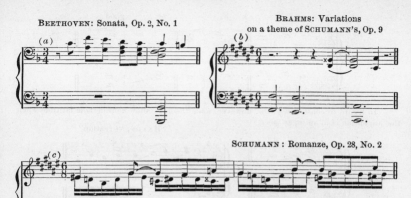

211. Suspensions generally occur on an accented beat, or on the accented portion of a beat, the resolution being unaccented;

but it is not necessary that such should be the case, for the following are true suspensions, though unaccented:

212. As a suspended tone is merely a temporary substitute for the harmonic tone that follows it, no progression which would be incorrect without a suspension is justified by its presence. *Care should therefore be used in leading another voice in similar motion to the tone of resolution.* The 8ves and 5ths in (*a*) and (*b*) are quite as bad as they would be in (*c*) and (*d*).

In regard to consecutive 5ths, however, some theorists allow considerable latitude when the suspension is in an inner voice.

It is seen that the effect in the extract from Haydn is softened by the predominance of the 7ths; the first example is not recommended.

213. As the dissonant element is of prime importance, a really good suspension should form a dissonance of a 7th, a 2d, or a 9th (the same as a 2d in the octave above) with some one of the integral tones of the chord; *e.g.:*

Suspensions without this element are generally weak and without character, although good where they occur interspersed with other stronger ones (§ **224**), *e.g.:*

The leading of the voices may result in a suspension to the 3d without the presence of one of the dissonances[1] mentioned above; this is good, even if not so strong as it might be;

[1] Some theorists have maintained that what we call the perfect 4th, while not a dissonance, is still not a perfect consonance, as it does not give a feeling of finality. Fétis goes so far as to make yet another subdivision for it in classification, under the name of "mixed consonance." This question is worth looking up by the student. One thing is clear, that the 4th in the example given does demand a resolution downward quite as decidedly as would a 7th.

it may be changed thus, if preferred.

In this connection the difference should be clearly understood between a note held over as the preparation of a secondary 7th chord, and a real suspension. In the former case we can always classify the factors as 1, 3, 5, 7, and the resolution is to a new chord (§ 219); *in the latter the suspension forms no part of the chord and is resolved while the rest of the chord remains (but cf § 216), e.g.:*

Not a real suspension.   Suspension to 3d.

NOTE. — It is questionable whether the so-called suspensions of the chord of the 9th (§ § 157–161, Ex. 2, 3, 6, 8b, and § 165, Ex. a) should be regarded as genuine ones; for it can be reasonably argued that the 9th does form an integral part of the suspended chord, and that the definition and idea of suspension are not strictly carried out. The chord of the 9th may in such cases be perhaps more properly said to be prepared, as chords of the 7th are prepared.

214. Practically the only subtle point in the treatment of suspensions is to know just when the tone of resolution may be anticipated in some other voice. For the student it is safe to say that such anticipation should generally be avoided; although here, as in other matters, there is a great difference between strict four-part writing for voices and free instrumental music. There is, however, a great difference of treatment between suspensions before the third and those before the root. The rule as to non-anticipation of the tone of resolution is also much stricter when the suspension (especially of the third) is in the bass, than when in the other voices; *e.g.* the following should never be written,

With the suspension to the root in the bass we sometimes find passages like the following:

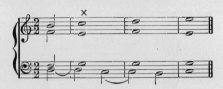

although the effect is somewhat harsh.

An analogous passage is cited from Beethoven, in which a tone of resolution in an inner voice is anticipated in the soprano, *e.g.*:

BEETHOVEN: Mass in D

215. The resolution to the root in the soprano is often anticipated in any one of the other voices, even in an inner one, *e.g.*:

Care should be taken to have this anticipation at least *nine degrees distant from the tone of suspension; the two tones should never appear simultaneously within the same octave, e.g.:*

With a suspension before a 3d, the 3d may often be anticipated in a lower voice, provided that the anticipation be nine degrees distant from the suspension.

the following quotation is a case in point.

BEETHOVEN : Sonata, Op. 14, No. 1

Such combinations as these, however, would be entirely erroneous:

When a suspension takes place before the leading tone, the latter, for an obvious reason, should never be anticipated.

216. At the same time that the suspension resolves, the rest of the harmony may be changed by chromatic alteration, or by various means which do not interfere with the suspension itself, *e.g.*:

on this point a study of the overture to *"Die Meistersinger"* will be profitable.

217. The suspended tone may even abandon its resolution altogether, and be merged in the following harmony; it also is occasionally resolved chromatically, *e.g.*:

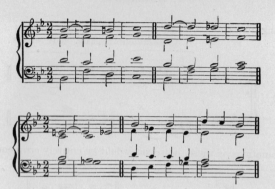

218. The resolution of a suspension is often delayed by the interpolation either of other tones belonging to the chord, or of passing or auxiliary tones which form an embellishment to the tone of resolution, *e.g.*:

BEETHOVEN: Sonata, Op. 10, No. 1

219. Suspensions are often used in more than one voice at a time; in fact all the parts but one may be held over. Triple suspensions are frequent in the authentic cadence, both in introducing the 6–4 chord and before the final tonic chord, *e.g.:*

On looking back, the analogy will be seen between the following suspensions and chords of the 9th, 11th, and 13th.

Quadruple Suspension.   Quintuple Suspension.

NOTE. — A succession of inversions of chords of the 7th may occur, in which at first sight we seem to have a series of suspensions;

these, however are not genuine suspensions (§ **213**).

220. The student will acquire indispensable practice by making out for himself a table of all possible suspensions before the factors of triads, and of seventh and ninth chords, in different positions and in various voices. A few of the most frequent suspensions are herewith given and also some of the less usual combinations.

221. Suspensions before the root of a triad from above and below.

222. Suspensions before the third of a triad from above.

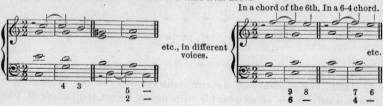

223. Suspensions before the third of a triad from below are rather rare; nevertheless they are perfectly possible and sometimes of striking effect, *e.g.*

224. Suspensions to the 5th of a triad from above are weak and seldom used except in connection with other genuinely dissonant suspensions (§ 213).

Suspensions to the 5th from below are often of great value, especially in the case of 7th chords; in (*a*) and (*b*) the G is a 5th (or, inverted, a 4th below) from C, the root.

225. Before the intervals of a dominant 7th chord, suspensions both from above, and in a somewhat less degree from below, are very effective and much used. A table is easily made out. A few models are given.

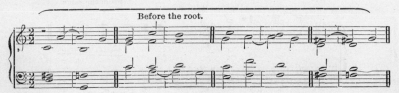

For suspensions before the third of a dominant 7th chcrd, *cf.* the preceding table of triads (§§ 222–223).

Before 3d from below.

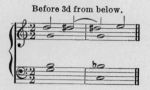

226. Suspensions before the 5th of a dominant 7th are much stronger than in the case of a plain triad, and are very frequent.

Chromatic resolution.

227. Suspensions before the 7th itself have to be handled with considerable skill in order that a genuine dissonant effect may be produced. At best, suspensions before the interval of a 7th are stronger in connection with a diminished 7th chord than with a dominant 7th.

228. Suspensions before the different factors of diminished 7th chords, of chromatically altered chords, and of all the augmented chords, are good and of frequent occurrence. The following quotation will illustrate these and other effects.

WAGNER: "Tannhäuser"

From the same

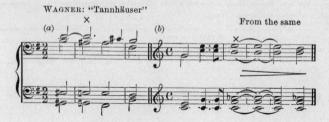

CÉSAR FRANCK

col 8va.

In the following of Chopin we have suspensions in the other voices, with a pedal bass: the entire passage repays study.

CHOPIN: Barcarolle, Op. 60

VERDI: "Aida," (Finale of Act 2)

etc.

In the above interesting passages we find augmented harmonies qualified by suspensions. The following quotations show a bold use of suspensions.

TSCHAIKOWSKI: 6th Symphony, last movement

etc.

CHAPTER XLII.

229. (In 6–10 the × indicates where a suspension is intended; the same sign is employed in a few instances with the soprano melodies, but suspensions are to be used in these in many cases where there is no ×. Do not confuse true suspensions with prepared chords of the 7th.)

13. (Chant) Close———

In c.

In A♭.

14. *Allegretto*

In ♭♭———In D♭.

15. (Hymn-tune)

In B♭.

In c.   In g.

EXERCISES FOR THREE VOICES

25.

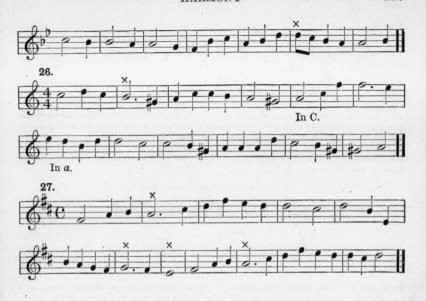

CHAPTER XLIII

ORNAMENTAL TONES

PASSING—TONES: AUXILIARY TONES: CHANGING TONES: APPOGGIATURAS: ANTICIPATION: MELODIC FIGURATION

230. THE PASSING-TONE has been defined (§§ **103, 147**). It may be diatonic (*a*), or chromatic (*b*) (*c*), accented (*c*), or unaccented (*a*) (*b*); the two tones between which it occurs may belong to the same or to different chords.

The interval to be filled out melodically may require more than one passing-tone (*d*) (*e*); these tones may also occur in two or three voices simultaneously (*e*).

By some theorists, the passing-tones in (e) would be considered as forming *passing chords*; this, however, is purely a question of definition. The same is true when auxiliary tones or appoggiaturas occur in several voices (§§ 232, 234, 235).

231. In § 103, it is said that no consecutive 8ves or 5ths may be allowed to result from passing-tones. It should, however, be pointed out that such 5ths do sometimes occur in the music of great composers: *e.g.*

MENDELSSOHN : Chorale in " St. Paul "

Such cases are to be regarded as exceptions. When these 5ths are accidentally made, it is possible and better to change the passage, even though the error be a purely technical one; *e.g.* (a) changed as in (b).

232. THE AUXILIARY TONE (§ 104) is unaccented, and proceeds upward or downward from its principal tone by a major or minor second (a), returning to that tone; it may also occur in two or three voices simultaneously (b) (§ 230).

When it is below the harmonic tone, it may be chromatically altered without affecting the harmonic progression (c); not so if it be above the harmonic tone (d). At (e) we have what looks like an exception, but G is really not an altered tone, as we here are using the form of the minor scale without leading-tone (§§ 22, 64).

The following is not an auxiliary tone, but an appoggiatura, being accented.

233. THE CHANGING TONE is an unaccented tone foreign to the chord with which it appears, and not necessarily a part of the following chord (*a*); it usually moves over a skip of a 3d (*b*).

234. THE APPOGGIATURA is defined in § **156**; it is a tone foreign to the chord with which it occurs, and enters by step or by skip. It may enter from above or below, and moves a 2d up or down, diatonically or chromatically, being either accented or (occasionally) unaccented; it is most often of the same length as the tone which it precedes, but may also be either shorter or longer than the latter; it may appear in any voice, and indeed, in two or three voices at the same time (§ **230**). IT DIFFERS FROM THE SUSPENSION IN NOT BEING PROLONGED FROM THE PRECEDING CHORD.

It may appear as an altered tone in one voice against the same tone unaltered in another voice.

Consecutive 5ths like the following, produced by appoggiaturas, are found in the works of the great composers, and are unobjectionable in their effect.

In the next illustration we have what may be properly termed a double appoggiatura.

In the familiar Rondo of Weber's Sonata, Op. 24, there are many passing-tones and appoggiaturas.

235. In the following examples of appoggiaturas (×) in an inner voice we see how freely they may enter; the resulting harshness is atoned for by our satisfaction in their resolution.

Passages like the following are easily explained as containing appoggiaturas in more than one voice (or appoggiatura chords, if that name be preferred.)

CHOPIN: Nocturne, Op. 15, No. 1

The ornaments so common in pianoforte music of the time of Bach (*cf.* his Suites and Partitas) can generally be explained as derived from the above ornamental tones. The trill, *e.g.* is nothing but the repetition of a group with an auxiliary tone.

236. THE ANTICIPATION (the opposite of suspension) is made by an unaccented tone, usually shorter in value than the following one, which moves to its appropriate tone in the next chord in advance of the other voices. It may also occur in two or three voices at the same time; but when all four voices move to the next chord in this manner, the effect is rhythmic and not harmonic, and we do not have a real anticipation.

A voice may anticipate by first moving to a tone of the new chord different from the one to which it finally goes (see the example from Grieg.)

237. MELODIC FIGURATION: by this term is understood the embellishment of a melody in any voice by the employment of the various non-harmonic tones with which we have been dealing, as well as of harmonic tones (*e.g.* the arpeggio). Scale passages, being extensions of groups of passing-tones, are much used. Excellent examples will be found in the slow movements of Beethoven's 5th and 9th symphonies, in the second theme of the slow movement of Schubert's Fantasie, Op. 78, and in the slow movement of his sonata, Op. 42.

238. PASSING-TONES: there are good illustrations of these in Schumann's Fantasie, Op. 17, second movement (especially in measures 50–57), and in the last movement of Mendelssohn's Italian Symphony.

AUXILIARY TONES: examples of these may be found in Chopin's study, Op. 25, No. 6, in the last movement of Schubert's C Major Symphony, and in the last movement of Beethoven's Sonata, Op. 53.

CHANGING TONES: in the slow movement of Beethoven's Sonata, Op. 28, and in Schubert's Impromptu, Op. 142, No. 1, are examples of these tones; in Chopin's Study, Op. 10, No. 4, a very comprehensive treatment of them may be found.

BACH: Organ fugue in G minor

APPOGGIATURAS:

SCHUMANN: Novellette, Op. 21, No. 6

WAGNER: "Die Walküre" (Act 2)

In the first movement of Tschaikowski's B minor symphony, just before the second theme enters in B major, there is a remarkable exhibition of the expressiveness that can result from the appoggiatura. See also the finale of "Tristan und Isolde," which is full of interesting suspensions and appoggiaturas.

ANTICIPATION:

HÄNDEL: Chorus, "His yoke is easy" ("Messiah")

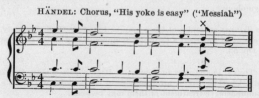

The following is an unusual example of a melody and its figuration going on simultaneously.

239. All music comes from the scale and the chord, however much that fact may be disguised by diatonic or chromatic ornamental tones; and scale passages, in final analysis, are found to have chords for their harmonic foundation. The thing to do is to first reduce every passage (which necessarily is based on some chords) to its simplest form.[1]

[1] A helpful little book towards understanding this question is Benjamin Cutter's "Harmonic Analysis" (Oliver Ditson Co.).

In analyzing compositions, the student is no longer to be restricted to such as are in four real parts. It is well to study other music also, establishing the harmonic outline, and defining the chord successions clearly; at present, songs for one voice with piano accompaniment, and the simpler kinds of piano pieces, will be of use. The ornamental tones so frequently present must not obscure understanding of the chord successions. The songs of Schubert, Schumann, Mendelssohn, Franz, and others, exist in cheap editions, as do the piano works of Mozart, Beethoven, Chopin, etc. No material is better for this especial study than the Mendelssohn "Songs without Words," for the melody is always simple and obvious, the real bass of every chord easily found, and the accompaniments sufficiently varied but not complex.

For an exhaustive study of part writing, and especially of suspensions and of chords of the 7th used in the freest possible manner, the student is referred to the 371 Vierstimmige Choralgesänge of Bach (Breitkopf und Härtel).

CHAPTER XLIV

240. EXERCISES INTRODUCING SUSPENSIONS, APPOGGIATURAS, PASSING-TONES, AUXILIARY TONES, CHANGING TONES, AND ANTICIPATION.

OBSERVE THAT IN SUSPENSIONS THE TONE APPEARS IN THE CHORD BEFORE, BUT DOES NOT DO SO IN APPOGGIATURAS. THE ABOVE DEVICES ARE INDICATED BY THE X, THOUGH THIS IS NOT SHOWN IN ALL CASES.

CHAPTER XLV

MODULATION

241. A musical composition of any length will be tedious if it remains throughout in the same key; some changes will be felt desirable. We therefore find that such are frequent in modern music;[1] at each time that one occurs a new tone is to be taken as the tonic for the time being,

---

[1] The music of Bach is so modern in the true sense of the word, that this term must be understood to cover the period of the last two hundred years at least; modern music is by no means only that produced yesterday, and indeed some of the latter is already antiquated to-day.

at the conclusion a return being nearly always made to the original
key. *The mere succession of different keys does not of itself constitute modulation.* For the definition of that term, and a few of the simplest examples, *cf.* § 108.

Modulation may be so fleeting as to seem barely to deserve the name
(for the general tonality of the following, *e.g.* is not affected by the chromatic
alterations of the chords);

or may be of a settled character. In the latter case, it must not only
take us definitely into a new key, but should keep us in that key long
enough to make us feel that a return to the former key, or a change to
another new key, will demand another distinct modulation.

242. In determining our key, we should not be misled by looking at one chord alone,
but must consider also the chords preceding and following. Take this chord, for instance:

the following examples show that, of itself, it does not fix the key in which we are.

A chromatically altered tone must not confuse us.

A MODULATION IS ALMOST ALWAYS PRODUCED BY INTRODUCING ONE OR
MORE TONES FOREIGN TO THE KEY IN WHICH WE ARE, AND BELONGING TO
THAT TO WHICH WE ARE GOING.   (*cf. note on page 233.*)

243. *It is of the utmost importance to understand at every point, where a change is made,
just what signature and what accidentals, if any, are indicated or implied.*   It is especially helpful to know thoroughly the signatures and accidentals (the latter resulting from leading-
tones) of the minor keys.

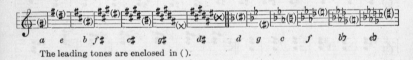

The leading tones are enclosed in ( ).

The student is advised to find what are the keys of the following scales.

Write the original chords of which the following are inversions, and find out in what key, or keys, each chord can occur.

(See the note on page 72.)

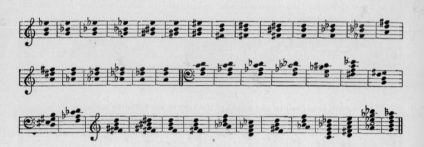

244. It is a helpful statement that "the nearest related keys to any major key are its dominant and sub-dominant, and the relative minors of these three keys; the nearest related keys to any minor key are its dominant and sub-dominant minors, and the relative majors of these three keys." (Prout.)

It must be understood that each of the modulations that follow is given as showing one of various ways; they are all made by the plainest and most definite means — by introducing the new tones foreign to the old keys, and concluding with an authentic cadence (generally including a 6-4 chord) in the new key. Refer to the modulations given in § **109**.

C to e.

C to *d*.

We can also modulate from C to G (I to V) and then to *e*, the relative minor of G; from C to F (I to IV) and then to *d*, the relative minor of F.

The diminished 7th, and the augmented 6, 6–5, and 6–4–3 chords are very useful (see later the modulations C major to E♭ major, *a* minor and *g* minor).[1]

245. Taking C for our tonic major, we can also modulate as follows: to D major by going to G, and then, taking G as a new tonic, modulating to D; to A major, by passing through *d* minor.

To E major, by a modulation to *a* minor and then to the dominant of the latter (E);

In this last modulation we notice the key-relationship of tonic and mediant. The term mediant relationship is now as well recognized as that of dominant relationship. This is also apparent in the keyrelationship of movements of symphonies, *cf.* Raff's "Lenore" symphony, the movements of which are respectively in the keys of E major, A flat major (enharmonic), C major, and *e* minor, with a final coda in E major.

Compare, later, the modulations to E♭ and A♭ major; to B major or *b* minor through a passing chord of *e* minor;

[1] The enharmonic use of augmented and dominant 7th chords as a means of modulation was spoken of in § **202**; see also §§ **112, 113, 121,** *e.g.*

The Liszt song referred to later in this chapter is **an** excellent illustration.

to F♯ major only by passing through other keys (*e.g. e* and *b* minor);

to B♭ major by going to F major, and then, taking the latter as a new tonic, modulating in the same way to B♭ major;

to E♭ major (the minor 3d above, and the relative major of the tonic minor of C);

to A♭ major (the major 3d below) through *f* minor;

to D♭ major, also through *f* minor;

to *a* minor, by means of an augmented chord (see page 85);

o *g* minor;

to *c* minor by means of the dominant 7th, common to both keys (p. 72);

to *f* minor in the same way as to F major; to *b♭* minor, through D♭ major. There is so little logical connection between C major and the keys of *f♯, c♯, g♯,* and *d♯, (e♭)* minor that a modulation to any of them can be effected only in a roundabout manner.

246. Taking *a* as our tonic minor (for the modulation to its relative major, *cf.* § 109) we can modulate:

to its dominant, E (major or minor);

to its sub-dominant *d* (minor);

to F major, its sub-mediant;

to G major;

to D major (through G major);
to A major in the smoothest way through *d* minor;   to B major (or *b* minor) its supertonic, through *e* minor;
to B♭ major through F major;
to E♭, A♭, D♭, G♭ (or F♯) major only through previous modulations;
to *f♯* minor through *b* minor;
to *c♯* and *g♯* minor through previous modulations;
to *g* minor;

Attention is called to the fact that, by means of a chord or chords *common to both keys*, a sufficiently decisive modulation can be made without the introduction of any notes foreign to the first of the two keys.

to *c* minor through *g* minor;

to *f* minor best through F major and *bb* minor;

to *eb* (*d#*) minor through previous modulations.

The examples of modulation given in this chapter are purposely of a simple and conventional sort; to make a comprehensive statement of more subtle methods would take too much space. For the very short passing modulations that are so frequent now-a-days, we by no means necessarily expect even the dominant chord of the new key, still less the dominant 7th or the 6–4 chord. It is occasionally the case that a new key is proceeded to without any modulation, or intermediate step, *e.g.*

SCHUBERT: Sonata, Op. 53 (Scherzo)

In Schubert we also note a fondness for unexpected alternations of tonic major and minor (Unfinished Symphony, slow movement).

CHANGES OF KEY WITHOUT MODULATION

247. Two of such changes are well known as being exceedingly effective — from a major key to a new tonic major downward by a major 3d, and to a new tonic major or minor upward by a minor 3d (see the preceding example by Schubert).

A notable instance of the former is in the last movement of Beethoven's 9th Symphony, just before the tenor solo; an example of the second change may be found in the last movement of the 1st Symphony of Brahms (page 92 of the score), the second chord in the latter being in a minor key.

Observe the enharmonic change at the ✕.

248. More subtle changes are seen in the following, in which chords between are elided; the effect would be an ordinary one were the elided chords sounded.

WAGNER: "Das Rheingold"

WAGNER: "Parsifal"

(With the elided chords.)

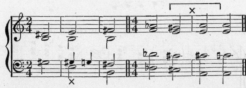

249. In these last examples also we have enharmonic changes. Enharmonic notation results from the fact that we can write notes as sharps, flats, naturals, double sharps, or double flats, as the case may be.

This notation is used chiefly for convenience, and often to avoid the use of too many or confusing accidentals; a beautiful enharmonic change may be found in the slow movement of Beethoven's 7th Symphony; see the last page of Liszt's D Flat Etude (No. 3 of "3 Etudes de Concert"); also Elsa's scene in the first act of "Lohengrin." (Scene 2, measures 9–13.)

ELGAR: "Dream of Gerontius"

WAGNER: "Siegfried," Act 3

BRAHMS: Ballade, Op. 10, No. 2.

WAGNER "Parsifal"

Observe in the following the differing notations in the voice and accompaniment, for ease in reading; also the perfectly good consecutive 5ths (see page 26).

FRANCK: "Les Béatitudes"

Augmented chords and dominant 7th chords may be interchangeable through enharmonic writing.

LISZT: Song, "Kennst Du das Land?"

250. The variety of enharmonic changes is endless, and the preceding gives the merest hint of what can be done in this direction.

In fact, the subjects of modulation and of change of key without modulation cannot be learned from a book; individual investigation through much reading of music, and experimenting, are the only ways by which one can hope to become acquainted with the possibilities.

It is advised that the following modulations be written out, and also improvised at an instrument.

G to D; D to e; Ab to c; F to e; Bb to d; b to G; e to d; f to Db; F# to e; Db to f#; E to F; g to Eb; B to G; f# to G; eb to Cb; Ab to bb; Eb to Cb; c# to A; f to Ab; B to g#.

CHAPTER XLVI

EXERCISES IN MODULATION

251. MARK the modulations (C, a, etc.); it is expected that suspensions and ornamental tones will be used. Passing-tones are indicated by slurs.

CHAPTER XLVII

CROSS RELATION (FALSE RELATION)

252. WHEN a tone of one chord occurs in another chord, in a different voice, chromatically altered, and so soon that the effect of the one tone has not passed from the mind before the other appears to contradict it with its chromatic alteration, we have a CROSS RELATION.[1]

[1] The following cannot be properly called a cross relation, for the A♮ is an appoggiatura, not affecting the tonality; some theorists include in the definition the simultaneous appearance of the altered and unaltered tone in the same chord.

In fact the cross relations produced by the appoggiaturas in the next illustration do not result in a bad effect.

Cf. Schumann's Andante and variations for two pianofortes.

It is difficult to lay down definite rules as to usage; the feeling of musicians has become so modified of late years that we may practically say that no cross relation is forbidden that sounds tolerably well.

253. The harshest form of it is when the 3d in a tonic triad is major and minor in different voices in two successive chords, the effect not being altered by the interposition of a passing-tone or of another chord:

for we almost get the feeling that two keys are used at the same time.

SCHUBERT: Impromptu, Op. 90, No. 1   BRAHMS: Symphony in F major

The capricious shifting between tonic major and minor is a characteristic of Schubert (*cf.* his song "Rosamonde"); in this illustration the effect is softened by the fact that E♭ is in the lower voice also, the change to E♮ taking place in that voice, § **254**); Brahms simply had two vital themes, which he intended to work together without regard to a temporary roughness.

254. The result is generally good when both the original and the altered tone occur in the same voice, as well as the altered tone in the other voice also (*a*), or (§ **138**) when the chromatically changed tone is a new leading-tone in a modulation (*b*). There are many cases where a cross relation sounds better than it looks upon paper; we sometimes, however, may prefer to avoid the effect by a change in one of the voices, for the sake of the slight improvement (*c*).

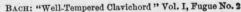

Liszt: Song, "Die Lorelei"

Bach: "Well-Tempered Clavichord" Vol. I, Fugue No. 2

CHAPTER XLVIII

SUGGESTIONS TO AID IN REVIEWING

255. The student must bear in mind that it is not enough simply to write down the exercises, even if that be done correctly. They must be listened to, and in playing them over the ear must try to disentangle the separate parts and to hear the individual voices. Writing exercises from figured basses serves in showing us how to think of chords and to notice the logical ways in which they succeed each other; the ability to harmonize soprano melodies and basses, without the aid of figures, is of utmost consequence. The student is also strongly advised to compose, from the very beginning of this review, some original basses and melodies to be harmonized.

256. The exercises are to be written with the voices on four separate staves; the C clefs are to be used to some extent. The exercises are also to be this time transposed a tone or semitone higher or lower, without exception. Besides playing them over, the student is advised to read them at the piano from the bass or soprano given, even though it is at first difficult to keep the progressions of the separate voices clearly in one's head.

Do not be mechanical; endeavor to be musical; aim at having an attractive and singable soprano and a varied and strong bass,[1] not neglecting good voice-leading in the alto and tenor; do not be satisfied with the first writing of an exercise, unless convinced that you cannot improve it. Open or close position is to be used as may seem best. We often change from one to the other several times in one exercise (pp. 42, 54, 137); this is not only done for variety, but may be necessary in order to avoid consecutive 8ves and 5ths. On the above points individual study and analysis of good choruses and part songs will be more helpful than advice.

Contrary motion is often more symmetrical than similar motion, where either is correct; contrary motion is generally to be preferred to similar motion, in approaching a dissonance.

As for spacing of the voices, it is safe to say that the limit of an 8ve should seldom be exceeded between soprano and alto, or alto and tenor; the bass may be even two 8ves distant from the tenor.

257. With Triads in Major Keys think of these two things, viz. consecutive 8ves and 5ths,[2] and the leading-tone (p. 29). With triads in major keys we meet with the interval of the augmented 4th, and in minor keys with those of the augmented 2d and 4th, such skips to be at present avoided as unvocal (pp. 39, 41, 42).

With both major and minor triads consider the question of doubling (generally the root), and the progressions from the second to the fifth and the fifth to the sixth triads; do not double the leading-tone except in sequences.

258. With Chords of the 6th we must ask when the bass is to be doubled, a thing as to which only very general directions can be given (p. 57). The 6-4 Chord is discussed at page 57; compare its use as a cadential and as a passing chord.

259. A statement of the usual treatment of the dominant 7th chord is at page 71,[3] and of its inversions at page 83; of the irregular resolutions at pages 93 and 105. As either root or 7th may be prolonged into the next chord, ascend, or descend, there is much detail. Some simple modulations are spoken of at page 85; a statement of passing-tones will be found at pages 77 and 138, and of auxiliary tones at page 78. These ornamental tones are to be used freely, but with discretion.

The dominant 7th has been used, from a purely musical point of view, too much in the exercises of this book, the intention being to get the student accustomed to the various ways in which it appears. The authentic cadence is stronger when the dominant triad is employed without the 7th. In reviewing, consider when that change is to be preferred, for variety if for no other reason.

---

[1] See page 63. A bass should move largely step-wise, although we may have even several moderate skips in succession; diminished skips are often good, augmented ones seldom; when a chord is repeated, it is sometimes well to have the bass skip an octave at the repetition; it is best not to return to the tonic unnecessarily often, as that produces monotony; two skips of a 4th or 5th in succession are generally to be avoided; cf. Spalding's "Tonal Counterpoint," pp. 24–38.

[2] An allowable license is that soprano and bass may sometimes move in consecutive 8ves in contrary motion, when the dominant is followed by the tonic triad (p. 74, top line).

[3] A unison followed by an 8ve, or 8ve followed by unison, produces the effect of consecutive 8ves, and is to be avoided. A unison followed by a 7th is equally bad, and a change in the leading of one of the other voices will remedy this defect, e.g.

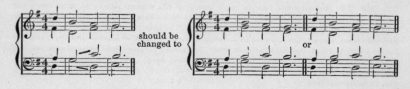

With the INVERSIONS OF THE DOMINANT 7TH chord we meet with the fact that consecutive 5ths are allowed, when one or both are not perfect (pp. 106, 108).

With the MODULATIONS occurring in exercises always look first of all for the leading tone of the new key; continue to transpose every exercise written.

260. CHORDS OF THE 7TH ON THE LEADING-TONE (pp. 114, 120); we again find both root and 7th with a variety of less usual resolutions; observe the ambiguity of the diminished 7th chords.

261. CHORDS OF THE 7TH ON OTHER DEGREES THAN V AND VII°; compare the strict rules for preparation (p. 132) with the hints as to free treatment (p. 128); remember that preparation is often desirable, even when unnecessary; there are many irregular resolutions. Generally speaking, we should try for a smooth leading of the voices. With SUCCESSIVE CHORDS OF THE 7TH in root position, be careful that the arrangement of the voices is good at starting (p. 136), as every alternate chord will be incomplete. INVERSIONS OF SECONDARY 7TH CHORDS, with their various resolutions, are described on page 142.

262. It has been said that passing and auxiliary tones should be used even in the simple triad exercises; with the secondary 7ths (if not before) introduce SUSPENSIONS and APPOGGIATURAS occasionally (p. 153). To have these latter, it will be necessary to change the figured bass or the soprano melody given; the exercises may also be altered to admit of the introduction of occasional CHROMATICALLY ALTERED CHORDS, AUGMENTED CHORDS, and, very sparingly, of CHORDS OF THE 9TH.

263. With the CHORD OF THE 9TH (p. 152) independent chords end, for practical purposes. In the discussion of CHORDS OF THE 11TH AND 13TH, however, it is recognized that examples such as those from "Die Meistersinger" forbid our dismissal of the claims of such chords to be considered independent; but the question cannot as yet be considered settled.

The fundamental points regarding SUSPENSIONS are plain. The suspended tone and the tone of resolution must be in the same voice; the tone of preparation is usually at least as long as that of suspension, and the tone of suspension is generally accented; no progression which would be incorrect without a suspension is justified by its presence; if the tone of resolution is anticipated in another voice also, the two tones must not be less than an 8ve apart; there is much detail. (p. 199.)

264. It will be of advantage to again write some EXERCISES WITH THREE VOICES; there is nothing that makes the harmonic structure so clear to the mind (pp. 43, 65, 80).

Finally — listen with eye and with ear to what you write.

If fresh exercises are desired for review work, the additional exercises to Emery's "Harmony" will be useful.

CHAPTER XLIX

THE PEDAL (PEDAL POINT, ORGAN POINT, POINT D'ORGUE)

265. THE PEDAL is defined as the sustaining of a tone or tones in one or more voices, while the other voices move through a succession of harmonies, some of which are foreign to the tone or tones forming the pedal.

The fact that a tone is sustained through harmonies, a few of which are slightly different, does not of itself always constitute a pedal; e.g. the introduction to "Das Rheingold" is not a pedal, in the true sense of the term. In one there must be harmonies frequently present that are entirely foreign to the sustained tone, i.e. dissonant from it.

266. The rules given by the older theorists differ so much from the practice of modern composers that a statement about the pedal, as it is used to-day, must be modified from that formerly given.

The important facts are these: (*a*) the pedal tone is practically always dominant or tonic; (*b*) chords of which the pedal can be considered as forming an integral part must alternate with foreign harmonies sufficiently often to produce a good logical effect; (*c*) the pedal tone is generally in the bass, but may occur in any of the other voices; (*d*) it is best for it to harmonize with the chords that begin and end the pedal, although there are exceptions to this.

267. We find the pedal on the dominant in the bass used very often to introduce the third portion, or at the very end of a sonata movement or of a fugue: *cf.* Beethoven, Op. 13, first movement; Op. 22, first movement; Op. 27, No. 2, last movement; Op. 53, first movement.[1] In the following is shown a pedal on the dominant, covering several octaves.

BEETHOVEN: Sonata, Op. 31, No. 2

268. The pedal in the bass on the tonic is also very much used. Remarkable examples of it may be found in the prelude to the great *a* minor organ fugue of Bach; at the end of the *c♯* minor fugue in Vol. I of the "Well-tempered Clavichord," and most striking of all — the introduction of the *c* minor symphony of Brahms. A double pedal in the bass, on tonic and dominant, has been employed; *cf.* Beethoven's "Pastoral Symphony,"

[1] The result is a pedal, even when the tone is not sustained, but (*a*) interrupted by rests (*b*) ornamented, as by an auxiliary tone, or (*c*) made part of a figure: (*a*) first movement of Beethoven, Op. 111; (*b*) last movement of Beethoven's 7th Symphony,

etc.; (*c*) first movement of Beethoven, Op. 53.

the waltz in the 3d act of "Die Meistersinger," the first movement of Brahms' F Major Symphony; attempts have even been made at constructing a triple pedal, but with no great success.

269. When the pedal is in the soprano it is called an *inverted pedal*. Excellent instances of this are in Mendelssohn's Overture, "Meeresstille und Glückliche Fahrt," and in the following:

WAGNER: "Flying Dutchman" Overture

as well as in Borodin's "Eine Steppenskizze aus Mittel-Asien," in which

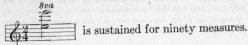 is sustained for ninety measures.

270. As an illustration of the pedal in inner voices, the following is given:

GRIEG: Pianoforte Concerto

271. In the introduction to "Die Walküre," and in the chorus, "But the righteous souls are in the hands of God," from the Brahms Requiem, will be found two of the most remarkable pedals in existence. The student is referred to the following as well worth examination:

Tschaikowski, first movement of 6th Symphony; Berlioz, "Ballet des Sylphes," from "La Damnation de Faust"; Beethoven, the ending of the Scherzo of the 5th Symphony; Brahms, last movement of f minor Sonata, Op. 5; Beethoven, introduction of Sonata, Op. 111, for a pedal in an inner voice; Schumann, 8th Novelette; Beethoven, the beginning of Op. 28; Schumann, finale of "Variations Symphoniques," Op. 13; Schumann, fugue on B-A-C-H, Op. 60, No. 1; Beethoven, first movement of string quartet Op. 59, No. 1, for a pedal in an inner voice; the introduction of Mendelssohn's 2d Organ Sonata, for the same; Brahms, Intermezzo, Op. 117, No. 1, for a pedal in the soprano; the song of Cornelius, "Ein Ton," for the same; Beethoven, the last movement of Sonata, Op. 109, for pedals in different voices; Mendelssohn's Variations, Op. 82, for modulation above a dominant pedal in the bass. As an example of a pedal simultaneously above and below the changing harmonies, the end of the slow movement of Beethoven's Sonata, Op. 10, No. 3.

272. Although pedals on other degrees of the scale are rare, they sometimes occur. Two good illustrations are in the second movement of Schumann's E flat Symphony (on the mediant), and in the following:

TSCHAIKOWSKI: 5th Symphony

273. It is of great consequence to remember this, that the voice next
above the pedal in the bass is generally to be regarded as the real bass,
chord progressions being made independently of the pedal tones; also,
although it is not to be stated as a fixed rule, it is well to aim at having
approximately every alternate chord such that the pedal tone can form a
part of it. No modulation that sounds well is forbidden, but extravagance
in that direction easily results in harshness.

274. The old rule that the pedal tone must be either tonic or dominant seems to indicate the Drone-bass as its origin. The Drone, in which the tonic is sustained as an accompany-
ing tone through a whole piece or large portion of a piece, is considered by some as the oldest
form of harmony. We hear it to-day from the Scottish bagpipes; two examples follow. It
will be observed that in these the nature of the piano does not permit such a tone to be indefinitely sustained, but that it must be repeated from time to time.

BACH: Gavotte in G minor
(Musette)

BACH: Gavotte in D minor
(Musette)

The Musette was an instrument of the bagpipe family; the second part **(Trio) of the**
Gavotte was sometimes written to imitate the effect of that instrument and was **given that**
name. A modern example is in the Gavotte of D'Albert's Suite, Op. 1, for piano.

EXERCISES WITH A PEDAL

275. Add the inner parts; aim at having a variety of chords; it is intended that **there**
shall be chromatically changed chords, augmented chords, suspensions, appoggiaturas, etc.

CHAPTER L

THE OLD MODES

276. THE ancient Greeks used in their music a number of MODES, as they are called; as no sharps or flats were employed, the simplest way to get an understanding of their effect is to play scales on the white keys of the piano, taking the different tones, C, D, E, F, G, A, B, as the starting, or principal tones.   The distribution of tones and semitones will not be the same as with our modern scales (with the exception of the mode beginning on C) and the use of the words key, keynote, and scale is inappropriate in this connection.

According to tradition, four of these modes were adopted by St. Ambrose at the end of the fourth century for use in the church, *viz.* the DORIAN, PHRYGIAN, LYDIAN and MIXOLYDIAN (beginning upon D, E, F, and G respectively); and two centuries later, St. Gregory the Great added four more, *i.e.* another series, beginning a 4th below the others. The first series was known as that of the Authentic Modes, and the second one as that of the Plagal Modes.[1]   Later researches, however, have made this statement of doubtful value.   An example of the manner in which these modes are harmonized for use in the Roman Church, in the book mentioned below, is here given.

277. These modes have not only been used in church music since the period referred to, but have been employed by composers of secular music to obtain distinctive effects.   As (with the exception of the one beginning upon C) they do not lend themselves to treatment according to our modern harmonic system, they can be appropriately harmonized best by the use of triads, with occasional chords of the 6th (*i.e.* without chords of the 7th), and do not permit our authentic cadence.   The effect produced by them is to our ears something antique; it is undoubtedly because of the refreshing contrast thus obtained that composers are now inclined to return occasionally to their use.

278. In old Gaelic, English, Russian, Polish music, etc., we see that the modes also affected the popular songs.   It is, therefore, natural that some of the examples quoted later should be found in the works of *e.g.* Chopin, Tschaikowski, Dvořák, as these composers were influenced by the folk song.

[1] For a thorough discussion of the subject, the student is referred to "Plain Song Accompaniment," by Niedermeyer and d'Ortigue, translated by Wallace Goodrich, and published by Novello, Ewer & Co.

279. The illustrations given are in the following modes.   (Observe the different distribution of tones and semitones.)[1]

Händel employs the Dorian mode in the chorus "And I will exalt him," ("Israel in Egypt"),

[1] The reader is referred to the article "Musica Ficta" in "Grove's Dictionary." In music of the fifteenth and sixteenth centuries, the natural feeling which was being developed for what we now call the leading-tone caused some accidentals to be written in, while others were supposed to be supplied by the singer at his discretion, so that some of the old modes were thus far modified. In modern music we sometimes find simply a partial or temporary use of an old mode in a composition written in other respects according to our present scale system. (*e.g.* Dvořák, Quartet Op. 96.)

and has taken the Phrygian mode for the first measures of the fugue "Egypt was glad when they departed," in the same oratorio.

In Beethoven's quartet in A minor, Op. 132, one movement is headed "Song of Gratitude, in the Lydian mode, offered to the Divinity by a Convalescent."

This mode is used by Chopin in his Mazurka, Op. 24, No. 2.

(Phrygian: observe the beautiful change to our modern scale of E major at measure 3.)

Dvořák: Symphony, "From the New World"
(Æolian, with E for starting tone)

Japanese National Hymn.   (Dorian)

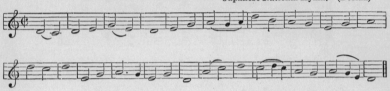

HARMONY OTHER THAN WITH FOUR VOICES

280. Through natural development, and from custom, harmony in four parts has come to be considered normal: we usually have a quartet of voices, a quartet of stringed instruments, a quartet of wood-wind instruments in the orchestra, etc.   It will now be well for the student to acquaint himself with such new points as arise when more or less than four voices are used.   To this end study of the chapter on this subject in Prout's "Harmony" is recommended, and the following works will repay thorough analysis: Bach, "St. Matthew Passion Music"; Brahms, "Triumphlied"; Händel, "Israel in Egypt"; Hubert Parry, "De Profundis" (for twelve voices); Strauss, "Two Anthems," Op. 34 (for sixteen voices); instrumental sextets and octets by Mendelssohn, Schubert, and Brahms.

ADDITIONAL EXERCISES

Page 37.

Triads in major keys.

20*d*. Open. Close. V I VI

20*e*. Open. Close. Open. VI VI III

20*f*. Close. Open. Close. IV—— VI

Page 47.

Triads in minor keys.

36*a*. Close. Open. VI V 6/4

36*b*. Close. Open. Close. In f♯ VI

36*c*. I I 6

36*d*. Close. Open. Close. VI 6/4

36*e*. Close. Open. Close. VI III+ 6 6 6/4 VI

Page 65.

31*a*. Open. 6 6/4 VI 6 6 6/4

31*b*. Open. Close. 6 6 III

31*c*. 6 I 6 6 6 6 6/4

31*d*. 6 6 VI 6 6/4

31*e*. 6 6 6/4 IV 6 6 6/4

Page 82.

Page 92.

INDEX

INDEX

ARTHUR FOOTE

TEXT BOOKS
Net

MODERN HARMONY IN ITS THEORY AND PRACTICE
By Arthur Foote and Walter R. Spalding $1.50
KEY TO THE 501 EXERCISES IN MODERN HARMONY 1.50
MODULATION AND RELATED HARMONIC QUESTIONS 1.25
SOME PRACTICAL THINGS IN PIANO PLAYING
A Handbook for Students and Teachers .... .60

PIANOFORTE VOLUMES IN
SCHMIDT'S EDUCATIONAL SERIES

Vol.

2	Op. 27. 9 ETUDES FOR MUSICAL AND TECHNICAL DEVELOPMENT $1.00	
73	Op. 52. TWENTY PRELUDES 1.00	
281	FROM REST HARROW. Little Suite .... .75	
20	TWELVE DUETS ON FIVE NOTES .... .75	

Classical Works Edited by ARTHUR FOOTE

24	BACH, 15 Two-Voice Inventions ....$ .75	
85	BACH, First Year Bach. 20 Compositions .... .75	
168a-b	BEETHOVEN, 10 Selected Sonatas Two Books, each 1.00	
165	CLEMENTI, 10 Studies from the Gradus ad Parnassum .... .75	
176	CRAMER, 12 Selected Studies .... .75	
145	HANDEL, First Year Handel .12 Easy Compositions .75	
171a-b	MOZART, 9 Selected Sonatas .... Two Books, each 1.00	
78a-b	A COMPENDIUM OF HELLER'S PIANOFORTE STUDIES .... Two Books, each .75	
401	10 CLASSICAL PIECES. Compositions by Bach, Beethoven, Brahms, Franck, Handel, Rameau, Scarlatti and Schumann 1.00	
74	ETUDE ALBUM. A Collection of Etudes Selected and Arranged in Progressive Order 1.00	
17a-b	INSTRUCTIVE ALBUM. 22 Short Piano Pieces Two Books, each .75	
116	35 TWO-PART STUDIES for Independent Part-Playing .... .75	

THE ARTHUR P. SCHMIDT CO.

BOSTON: 120 Boylston St.   NEW YORK: 8 West 40th St.

THE FIRST YEAR SERIES
OF TEXT BOOKS

BY

THOMAS TAPPER, Litt. D.

FIRST YEAR MUSICAL THEORY

FIRST YEAR MELODY WRITING

FIRST YEAR HARMONY

SECOND YEAR HARMONY

FIRST YEAR ANALYSIS (Musical Form)

FIRST YEAR COUNTERPOINT

FIRST YEAR MUSIC HISTORY

FROM PALESTRINA TO GRIEG
(First Year Music Biography)

THE ARTHUR P. SCHMIDT CO.

BOSTON
120 Boylston St.

NEW YORK
8 West 40th St.